# THE
# A-LIST
# SAT COURSE
# DRILL BOOK

The A-List SAT Course Drill Book
ISBN: 978-1-944959-10-4

A-List Education
29 W36 St, 7th Floor
New York, NY 10019
(646) 216-9187
www.alisteducation.com

# Table of Contents

# Course A

## 2 hr 24 hr

# Homework 1

## Reading: Main Idea Questions 1

Vegetarianism in on the rise in virtually all demographic groups in the United States and in much of the rest of the world. Even more impressive is the rate
Line of increase in the percentage of the U.S. population that
5 has substantially cut back on their animal product intake. These changes are not fads: analysts of every segment of the food industry agree that the American diet has irrevocably altered.

The reasons for this are many and overlapping.
10 Nutrition and animal well-being, not surprisingly, are the most often cited, but increasingly, recent converts to vegetarianism mention cost, weight loss, food safety, and religious proscriptions as motivating factors. Interestingly, the reason most often given by *non-*
15 *vegetarians* for why they choose to remain meat-eaters—taste—also plays a role in the decision of others to forego animal products. In the last ten years, food manufacturers have become more skilled at producing easy-to-prepare vegetarian items that simply taste
20 delicious.

**MAIN IDEA:** _____

_____

_____ **1.** The primary function of the first paragraph is to:

**ANTICIPATION:** _____

_____

A) briefly describe the how the food industry tracks vegetarianism.
B) explain that the United States has started a worldwide rise in vegetarianism.
C) show that the author approves in the rise in vegetarianism.
D) identify the trend that people in the United States eat less meat and will continue to do so.

_____ **2.** The main purpose of the second paragraph is to:

**ANTICIPATION:** _____

_____

A) give arguments in favor of the changes discussed in the first paragraph.
B) present an overview of a range of recent changes that have taken place in the American diet.
C) discuss changes in the manufacturing process of vegetarian meals.
D) provide possible explanations for the increase in vegetarianism.

CONTINUE ➤

# Reading: Main Idea Questions 2

A recent nationwide poll confirms what one hears daily from news media of every stripe: most Americans believe that the country is more polarized than at any time in recent history. Specifically, 81% of respondents said the country "definitely" or "almost certainly" more divided by social and political issues than it has been since the Civil War. Similarly, 89% agreed that political discourse has become more antagonistic in the last 50 years.

*Line 5*

While these results are clear enough, the question remains: are they right? Are we really that divided? The attempt to determine how well this appraisal reflects actual state of affairs has been elusive. This same survey found that while most people describing themselves as "politically conservative" agreed about the general meaning of that phrase, they were not nearly as much in agreement about specific policy issues. Even those who self-described as "very conservative" or "very liberal" shared significant views on a number of relevant issues. Measuring levels of antagonism is similarly difficult. Does one measure presidential vetoes or perhaps overturns of vetoes? The number of protests? Instances of violence?

*10*

*15*

*20*

**MAIN IDEA:** _____

_____

_____ **3.** What is the main idea of the first paragraph?

**ANTICIPATION:** _____

_____

A) The country is not nearly as divided as most people believe it to be.
B) Evidence shows a large majority of people believe the country is politically divided.
C) The news media has correctly predicted the attitudes of most Americans.
D) America has been becoming steadily more divided since the Civil War.

_____ **4.** What is the main idea of the second paragraph?

**ANTICIPATION:** _____

_____

A) Most people in the United States have more in common with each other than they realize.
B) Respondents did not correctly understand the meanings of the words they used to describe themselves.
C) Though the level of polarization in the United States is considerable, the apparent level of antagonism is overstated.
D) It is difficult to determine whether the country is really as polarized as people believe it to be.

CONTINUE ➤

# Math: Plug In

**DIRECTIONS: You must use Plug In** on each of the following questions. Write your answer in the space before the question number.

_____ **5.** Alan has $x$ chocolate bars and gets 10 more bars. He gives away half of his chocolate, and then gets another 10 bars. In terms of $x$, how many chocolate bars does Alan now have?

A) $x + 15$
B) $x + 20$
C) $\dfrac{x}{2}$
D) $\dfrac{x}{2} + 15$

_____ **6.** If $a$ is 5 less than twice $b$, which of the following gives $b$ in terms of $a$?

A) $2a - 5$
B) $5 + 2a$
C) $\dfrac{5 - a}{2}$
D) $\dfrac{a + 5}{2}$

_____ **7.** Stewart's car can hold a maximum of $g$ gallons in its gas tank, and gas costs $c$ dollars per gallon. If the car currently has 2 gallons of gas in the tank, what is the cost, in dollars, to fill up the rest of the tank?

A) $cg - 2$
B) $cg - 2c$
C) $cg - 2g$
D) $g - 2c$

_____ **8.** In a series of three numbers, the second number is 3 less than the first, and the third is three times the second. If the first number is $x$, how much greater than the second number is the third number?

A) $2x - 6$
B) $2x - 9$
C) $2x - 12$
D) $3x - 3$

_____ **9.** Olivia earns a commission of 15 percent of the price of every boat she sells. Which of the following gives the amount of her commission, in dollars, if she sells $x$ boats that each cost $y$ dollars?

A) $15xy$
B) $1500xy$
C) $\dfrac{3xy}{20}$
D) $\dfrac{3y}{20x}$

**STOP**

# Homework 2

## Reading: Passage 1

Most people use the word "hobo" as little more than a derogatory term for the homeless, deriding them as lazy bums who spend their days idly wandering the country. However, the word properly refers to an itinerant worker. Far from lazy, hobos travel hundreds of miles looking for any work they can find. When jobs were especially scarce during the Great Depression several hundred thousand hobos traveled from town to town, hitching rides in railway freight cars and carrying only the bare essentials on their backs. As their numbers increased, hobo culture became more organized, developing ways to communicate with each other to keep safe. These included homemade travel books and a system of written symbols to inform other hobos whether nearby houses were friendly or hostile. Today, hobos even have their own union and an annual convention in Britt, Iowa, home of the National Hobo Museum.

*Line 5*

*10*

*15*

MAIN IDEA: _____

_____

_____ 1. In context, the author includes lines 1-4 ("Most… country") in order to

ANTICIPATION: _____

_____

A) present a common opinion the author will refute
B) demonstrate the proper connotation of a word
C) disparage the indolence of the hobo lifestyle
D) detail the history of itinerant workers in the U.S.

_____ 2. The "books" (line 13) and the "system" (line 14) are given as examples of

ANTICIPATION: _____

_____

A) objects that can be seen in the National Hobo Museum
B) the dangers that hobos can encounter on the road
C) methods hobos use for interacting with their peers
D) tools needed to perform a typical job that a hobo finds

CONTINUE →

# Reading: Passage 2

Americans are spoiled by the mutual intelligibility of the regional variations of their language. The differences between dialects within the country are
*Line* trivial, such as whether a carbonated beverage is called
5 "soda" or "pop" or whether "caramel" should be pronounced with two syllables or three. When compared with other languages, American English shows astonishing little variation. In Germany, for example, there are over a dozen distinct Germanic languages
10 spoken, from Alemannic to Westphalian, some of which have deep grammatical differences beyond simple vocabulary or phonology. The difference can be starker with German spoken in other countries: the "German" spoken in Switzerland is practically incomprehensible to
15 one who speaks only Standard German. When Americans travel in America, other people may sound funny, but they understand each other. If a German strays too far from home, the people around him might as well be speaking Latin.

**MAIN IDEA:** _____

_____

_____ **3.** The author says Americans are "spoiled" (line 1) because they

**ANTICIPATION:** _____

_____

A) struggle to learn many different varieties of American English
B) use different words for common things than people from other parts of the country
C) have little difficulty understanding each other compared with people in other countries
D) speak a language that has no variation across the country

_____ **4.** In line 19, "Latin" serves as an example of a language that

**ANTICIPATION:** _____

_____

A) has significant dialectical variation
B) is a dialect spoken within Germany
C) only varies in simple vocabulary and phonology
D) is so foreign that it is incomprehensible

CONTINUE ➤

# Math: Backsolve

**DIRECTIONS: You must use Backsolve** on each of the following questions. Write your answer in the space before the question number.

_____ **5.** Tree X is 23 inches tall and tree Y is 73 inches tall. Tree X grows 5 inches a year and tree Y grows 3 inches a year. In how many years will tree X be the same height as tree Y?

A) 10
B) 15
C) 25
D) 30

$$a + b = 17$$
$$b + c = 35$$
$$a + c = 28$$

_____ **8.** In the system of equations above, what is the value of $a$?

A) 5
B) 10
C) 12
D) 24

_____ **6.** At a movie theater, small drinks cost $3 each and large drinks cost $5 each. The theater sells 100 total drinks for a total of $380. How many small drinks were sold?

A) 45
B) 50
C) 55
D) 60

_____ **9.** Molly has 36 more red shirts than blue shirts. Half the number of red shirts equals twice the number of blue shirts. How many blue shirts does she have?

A) 9
B) 12
C) 24
D) 36

$$B(d) = 2d^2 + 10$$

_____ **7.** The function $B$, defined above, models the number of new bees born in a beehive after $d$ days. According to this model, how many days would it take for the colony to gain 108 new bees?

A) 4
B) 5
C) 6
D) 7

CONTINUE

# Math: Technique Review

**DIRECTIONS: You must use an SAT math technique** on each of the following questions. You must indicate which technique you used—either **Plug In** or **Backsolve**—and show your work.

_____ 10. Alvin, Barney, and Cedric made a total of 18 sandwiches to bring to a picnic. Alvin made 2 more sandwiches than Barney made, and Cedric made 3 times as many as Alvin. How many sandwiches did Barney make?

   A)   2
   B)   4
   C)   6
   D)   10

_____ 11. Technique used:

   A)  Plug In
   B)  Backsolve

_____ 12. If Arthur was $y$ years old exactly 3 years ago, how old will he be in exactly $x$ years?

   A)  $x + y$
   B)  $x + y - 3$
   C)  $x - y - 3$
   D)  $x + y + 3$

_____ 13. Technique used:

   A)  Plug In
   B)  Backsolve

_____ 14. The high road to Scotland is 180 miles longer than the low road. When Jocelyn goes to Scotland by the high road and returns along the low road, the round trip is 1,060 miles. How many miles is the high road?

   A)  350
   B)  440
   C)  530
   D)  620

_____ 15. Technique used:

   A)  Plug In
   B)  Backsolve

_____ 16. If $a$, $b$, and $c$ are consecutive even integers such that $a < b < c$, which of the following is equal to $a^2 + b^2 + c^2$?

   A)  $3b^2 + 2$
   B)  $3b^2 + 6$
   C)  $3b^2 + 8$
   D)  $3b^2 + 6b + 5$

_____ 17. Technique used:

   A)  Plug In
   B)  Backsolve

_____ 18. It takes Donna 4 minutes to grade an essay, and it takes Clay 6 minutes to grade an essay. If they both start working at the same time, how many minutes will it take them to grade 20 total essays?

   A)  40
   B)  48
   C)  72
   D)  100

_____ 19. Technique used:

   A)  Plug In
   B)  Backsolve

**STOP**

# Homework 3

## Writing: Verbs 1

_____ 1. My best friend, who enjoys making music and plays several instruments, <u>plan</u> to visit Maine this winter and write songs in a cabin.

1. A) NO CHANGE
   B) have planned
   C) are planning
   D) plans

_____ 2. When they worked together at the library, Naomi and Nicholas <u>hunt</u> through the aisles for books with ridiculous names.

2. A) NO CHANGE
   B) will hunt
   C) would hunt
   D) are hunting

_____ 3. It looks like our hike might be cut short because a swarm of angry bees <u>have blocked</u> the trail ahead.

3. A) NO CHANGE
   B) is blocking
   C) would block
   D) are blocking

_____ 4. In 1965, Soviet cosmonaut Alexey Leonov <u>will perform</u> the first extra-vehicular space walk in human history.

4. A) NO CHANGE
   B) performs
   C) performed
   D) has performed

_____ 5. The dulcet tones of the piano that had been drifting across the restaurant to the table where Danny waited for his date <u>were</u> suddenly drowned out by the sound of a blender running in the kitchen.

5. A) NO CHANGE
   B) has been
   C) was
   D) is

CONTINUE

**Name:** _____  **Date:** _____

# Writing: Verbs 2

_____ 6. In Professor Tomlin's lab, a team of undergraduate students <u>have found</u> a way to "listen" to space by monitoring radio waves as they travel through the cosmic void.

6. A) NO CHANGE
   B) are finding
   C) find
   D) has found

_____ 7. Past the stone monument that marks the end of the beach, <u>lies</u> two tide pools that glitter beautifully in the moonlight.

7. A) NO CHANGE
   B) lie
   C) has lied
   D) is

_____ 8. Next spring, the Emergency Response Team created by the previous mayor <u>has been</u> replaced by a smaller Emergency Dispatch Service that will direct existing resources to respond to crises.

8. A) NO CHANGE
   B) was
   C) is
   D) will be

_____ 9. The requests that Joanna's employees made—on a number of topics but most notably for more vacation time—<u>were</u> reasonable, so she happily changed her policies.

9. A) NO CHANGE
   B) would be
   C) was
   D) is

_____ 10. Because it <u>had been containing</u> private details about his own life and family, Eugene O'Neill's masterpiece *A Long Day's Journey Into Night* was not published until after his death.

10. A) NO CHANGE
    B) contained
    C) will contain
    D) has contained

CONTINUE ➤

# Writing: Pronouns 1

_____ 11. All the apartments in the new buildings have a new washing machine for the convenience of <u>it's</u> occupants.

11. A) NO CHANGE
    B) their
    C) its
    D) there

_____ 12. I thought this coat looked great on me at the store, but when I got home I found that <u>it's</u> not exactly the color I expected.

12. A) NO CHANGE
    B) its
    C) its'
    D) they're

_____ 13. Ian loved the look of his new phone, but disliked <u>its'</u> lack of features.

13. A) NO CHANGE
    B) their
    C) its
    D) it's

_____ 14. Every meeting of the Iowa Misanthrope Club ends with a vote for a new chairperson, <u>whom</u> would be forced to host the next meeting.

14. A) NO CHANGE
    B) who
    C) which
    D) whose

_____ 15. If one wishes to build a successful business, <u>they</u> should carefully consider how to stand out from competing ventures.

15. A) NO CHANGE
    B) we
    C) you
    D) one

CONTINUE

# Writing: Pronouns 2

_____ **16.** The school's new policy allows students to easily obtain a copy of <u>their</u> attendance or academic records at any point during the year.

**16.** A) NO CHANGE
B) his or her
C) they're
D) your

_____ **17.** Paul and Olivia liked how <u>they're</u> new back yard opened up directly to a meadow with a tiny stream.

**17.** A) NO CHANGE
B) its
C) there
D) their

_____ **18.** The hippopotamus, despite having an innocuous appearance, is actually extremely dangerous and can kill with <u>their</u> powerful bite.

**18.** A) NO CHANGE
B) they're
C) its
D) it's

_____ **19.** Scientists at NASA are planning a mission to bring an asteroid into lunar orbit so <u>they</u> can be studied more easily by astronauts.

**19.** A) NO CHANGE
B) it
C) which
D) them

_____ **20.** After the conclusion of the piano recital, the teacher asked <u>my friend and I</u> to play a duet together as the audience left the auditorium.

**20.** A) NO CHANGE
B) my friend and me
C) I and my friend
D) my friend and myself

CONTINUE

# Math Fundamentals Review

_____ **21.** If $\dfrac{a}{2} \times \dfrac{1}{8} = \dfrac{\frac{3}{4}}{6}$, then $a = ?$

A)  2
B)  3
C)  4
D)  6

_____ **22.** What is the remainder when 52 is divided by 3?

A)  0
B)  1
C)  2
D)  3

_____ **23.** A recipe calls for 3 cups of flour for every 5 cups of sugar. If Bill uses 15 cups of flour, how many cups of sugar should he use?

A)  10
B)  15
C)  20
D)  25

_____ **24.** A certain park contains only maple and elm trees in a ratio of 2 to 3, respectively. If there are a total of 40 trees, how many elm trees are there in the park?

A)  16
B)  18
C)  20
D)  24

_____ **25.** What percent of 40 is 8?

A)  5
B)  10
C)  20
D)  30

_____ **26.** 9 is 15 percent of what number?

A)  60
B)  70
C)  75
D)  80

_____ **27.** Joe made 160 dollars last week and 180 dollars this week. What was the percent increase in his pay?

A)  10
B)  12.5
C)  15
D)  17.5

_____ **28.** $x^3 \left( x^2 \right)^5 = ?$

A)  $x^5$
B)  $x^7$
C)  $x^{10}$
D)  $x^{13}$

_____ **29.** If $d^3 \times d^4 = d^p$ and $\dfrac{d^{12}}{d^6} = d^q$, what is $p + q$?

A)  1
B)  6
C)  7
D)  13

_____ **30.** If $|x - 6| = 23$, which of the following gives all possible values of $x$?

A)  $-29$
B)  $-17$
C)  $-17$ and $29$
D)  $17$ and $-29$

**STOP**

# Homework 4

## Writing: Fragments 1

_____ 1. Waffles, though primarily served at breakfast in America, <u>but eaten</u> throughout the day in Belgium.

1. A) NO CHANGE
   B) eaten
   C) are eaten
   D) eating

_____ 2. The launch of the new <u>website, already delayed</u> three weeks when the developers were forced to postpone it indefinitely.

2. A) NO CHANGE
   B) website; it was already delayed
   C) website was already delayed
   D) website, which was already delayed

_____ 3. Nepal's national <u>flag, which is the world's only non-rectangular national flag and also</u> the only flag that is taller than it is wide.

3. A) NO CHANGE
   B) flag, which is the world's only non-rectangular national flag and which is
   C) flag, the world's only non-rectangular national flag, as well as
   D) flag is the world's only non-rectangular national flag and also

_____ 4. The northern cardinal, <u>one of the most common birds in North America, and also</u> the official bird of seven different U.S. states.

4. A) NO CHANGE
   B) one of the most common birds in North America, is
   C) which is one of the most common birds in North America and
   D) which is one of the most common birds in North America and is

_____ 5. Harry Beck's landmark 1931 map of the London Underground rail <u>system depicting</u> train lines only in straight lines with orthogonal angles, with no reference to actual geography or topology.

5. A) NO CHANGE
   B) system depicted
   C) system that depicted
   D) system; it depicted

CONTINUE ➤

# Writing: Fragments 2

_____ **6.** Dwayne Johnson, also known as The <u>Rock, who has</u> made a skillful transition from professional wrestler to Hollywood actor.

**6.**
A) NO CHANGE
B) Rock, having
C) Rock, and who has
D) Rock, has

_____ **7.** If the school's administrators are serious about increasing <u>enrollment. They</u> should take a hard look at where they're spending their money.

**7.**
A) NO CHANGE
B) enrollment, they
C) enrollment; they
D) enrollment,

_____ **8.** In Myanmar, the military <u>having excluded Aung San Suu Kyi,</u> the leader of the country's democratic movement, from holding the office of president.

**8.**
A) NO CHANGE
B) has excluded Aung San Suu Kyi,
C) having excluded Aung San Suu Kyi, who is
D) excluding Aung San Suu Kyi,

_____ **9.** Even though the forecast didn't call for <u>rain, Mary still packed</u> an umbrella for her vacation, knowing that the local climate was highly unpredictable.

**9.**
A) NO CHANGE
B) rain. Mary still packed
C) rain, Mary still packing
D) rain, but Mary still packed

_____ **10.** Descending deeper and deeper into the murky depths, Jordan Summers, the leader of the scuba diving tour, <u>while keeping</u> a close eye on the less experienced divers in her group.

**10.**
A) NO CHANGE
B) keeping
C) kept
D) who kept

CONTINUE

_____ 11. Andrew Johnson was impeached by the House of Representatives in <u>1868, then he was acquitted</u> in the Senate by one vote, allowing him to continue his term as President of the United States.

11. A) NO CHANGE
    B) 1868, he was acquitted
    C) 1868; acquitted
    D) 1868; however, he was acquitted

_____ 12. Despite their image as a quintessentially American fruit, apples were first cultivated in Kazakhstan in central Asia, <u>China is the largest apple producer today</u>.

12. A) NO CHANGE
    B) China produces apples in the largest number today
    C) and China is the largest apple producer today
    D) today it is China that produces the most apples

_____ 13. It had been twenty years since Shelly had visited her <u>hometown, she feared</u> what it had become in the time she was gone.

13. A) NO CHANGE
    B) hometown; she being afraid of
    C) hometown, and she feared
    D) hometown, therefore she feared

_____ 14. <u>Jeff initially did not feel prepared for the test,</u> he had no trouble with any of the questions once it started.

14. A) NO CHANGE
    B) Jeff's initial feeling was that he was not prepared for the test
    C) Initially, Jeff felt that he was not prepared for the test
    D) Although Jeff initially did not feel prepared for the test

_____ 15. Most people consider George Washington to be America's first President, but some argue it was technically John <u>Hanson, he was President of the Continental Congress</u> under the Articles of Confederation from 1781 to 1782.

15. A) NO CHANGE
    B) Hanson, who was President of the Continental Congress
    C) Hanson, the President of the Continental Congress was
    D) Hanson; President of the Continental Congress

CONTINUE →

# Writing: Run-Ons 2

_____ **16.** We have to bring a lot of equipment to the practice field <u>tomorrow it</u> would be easier to take my car.

**16.** A) NO CHANGE
B) tomorrow, it
C) tomorrow, therefore, it
D) tomorrow, so it

_____ **17.** Nina's new restaurant buys ingredients from local producers whenever <u>possible, however, some</u> foods just can't be grown outside of a tropical climate.

**17.** A) NO CHANGE
B) possible, some
C) possible; however, some
D) possible, nevertheless some

_____ **18.** <u>Tensions in Europe were rising on the eve of World War I, no one</u> could have predicted that the sovereignty dispute between Austria and Serbia would lead to a conflict that would embroil the whole continent.

**18.** A) NO CHANGE
B) Although tensions in Europe were rising on the eve of World War I, no one
C) Tensions in Europe had risen on the eve of World War I, no one
D) Tensions in Europe had risen on the eve of World War I, however no one

_____ **19.** Because Warren loved to swim, he decided to take his vacation in the <u>Caribbean, the water is</u> much clearer and warmer than those near his home in Virginia.

**19.** A) NO CHANGE
B) Caribbean, where the water is
C) Caribbean the water there can be
D) Caribbean, its waters are

_____ **20.** Terry Gross has been a staple for National Public Radio for over forty <u>years, her</u> show "Fresh Air" continues to be one of the network's most popular programs.

**20.** A) NO CHANGE
B) years, and her
C) years, it is her
D) years her

CONTINUE ➡

# Math: Algebraic Manipulation

_____ **21.** If $D = ST$, which of the following expressions gives $S$ in terms of $D$ and $T$?

   A) $S = DT$

   B) $S = \dfrac{D}{T}$

   C) $S = \dfrac{T}{D}$

   D) $S = \dfrac{D}{T^2}$

_____ **22.** Given the formula $V = \pi r^2 h$, which of the following expressions gives the height ($h$) of the cylinder?

   A) $h = \dfrac{V}{\pi r^2}$

   B) $h = \dfrac{\pi r^2}{V}$

   C) $h = \dfrac{\pi}{V r^2}$

   D) $h = \dfrac{1}{\pi r^2 V}$

_____ **23.** Given the formula $a = \dfrac{v - u}{t}$, what is $v$ in terms of $a$, $t$, and $u$?

   A) $v = \dfrac{u}{at}$

   B) $v = \dfrac{at}{u}$

   C) $v = u - at$

   D) $v = u + at$

_____ **24.** Given the formula $T = 2\pi\sqrt{\dfrac{L}{g}}$, what is $L$ in terms of $T$ and $g$?

   A) $L = \dfrac{4\pi r^2}{T^2 g}$

   B) $L = \dfrac{Tg}{2\pi}$

   C) $L = \dfrac{T^2 g}{4\pi^2}$

   D) $L = \dfrac{T^2 g}{2\pi^2}$

_____ **25.** The formula $F = \dfrac{9}{5}C + 32$ gives the temperature in Fahrenheit in terms of Celsius. Which of the following expression gives the temperature in Celsius in terms of Fahrenheit?

   A) $C = (F - 32)\dfrac{5}{9}$

   B) $C = (F - 32)\dfrac{9}{5}$

   C) $C = \dfrac{5}{9}F - 32$

   D) $C = \dfrac{9}{5}F + 32$

CONTINUE →

# Math: Systems of Equations

_____ **26.** What are the solutions for the equations
$-x + 2y = -10$ and $2 - 6y = 5x$ ?

A) $x = -4, y = 3$
B) $x = -3, y = 4$
C) $x = 3, y = -4$
D) $x = 4, y = -3$

_____ **27.** What values of $a$ and $b$ satisfy the system of equations below?

$$-3a - 9b = -15$$
$$7a - 3b = 59$$

A) $a = -8, b = 1$
B) $a = -1, b = 8$
C) $a = 8, b = -1$
D) $a = 8, b = 1$

_____ **28.** What values of $m$ and $n$ satisfy the system of equations below?

$$3m + 5n = -6$$
$$-2m + 7n = 4$$

A) $m = -2, n = -2$
B) $m = 0, n = -2$
C) $m = -2, n = 0$
D) $m = 2, n = 0$

_____ **29.** What values of $p$ and $q$ satisfy the system of equations below?

$$\frac{p - q}{2} = p + 3$$
$$p + 5 = q + 3$$

A) $p = -4, q = -3$
B) $p = -4, q = -2$
C) $p = -2, q = -4$
D) $p = 2, q = 4$

_____ **30.** What values of $c$ and $d$ satisfy the system of equations below?

$$5c - 5d = 5$$
$$4c - 3d = 13$$

A) $c = 10, d = 9$
B) $c = 9, d = 10$
C) $c = -9, d = 10$
D) $c = -10, d = -9$

**STOP**

# Homework 5

## Reading: Explicit Questions 1

*Gravitational waves* are changes in the curvature of space-time, moving at light-speed, that are initiated by accelerating bodies found within binary star systems.

*Line*
5 These bodies can be neutron stars, white dwarf stars, or black holes. When, for example, binary neutron stars orbit close to each other, the extremely large acceleration of their masses form gravitational waves. An observer would notice rhythmic (wave-like) distortions in local space-time. Distances between

10 objects would fluctuate with the frequency of the wave.

So do these waves actually affect Earth? The short answer is yes, but because of the astronomical distances involved, the effect is so minuscule that only the most sensitive devices can measure the effect. The first

15 observation of a gravitational wave was made on September 14th, 2015. Two black holes, each about 30 times more massive than our sun, had spiraled and merged, creating an unimaginably powerful wave that finally reached us after traveling through a billion light

20 years of space. By the time it got here, it was detected by a device whose 4-kilometer arm changed in length by the unimaginably small distance of ten-thousandths of the width of a proton.

MAIN IDEA: _____

_____

_____ 1. According to the passage, the gravitational wave that scientists were first able to observe was:

ANTICIPATION: _____

_____

A) created by an event that took place in 2015.
B) found within the orbit of neutron stars.
C) created through the interactions of two black holes.
D) measured to be approximately 4-kilometers long.

_____ 2. The passage states that the large acceleration of massive objects in space:

ANTICIPATION: _____

_____

A) can alter the way that space and time appear to behave.
B) can cause binary star systems to orbit each other more closely.
C) typically produce fluctuations in local space-time conditions that are observable from Earth.
D) are responses to curvatures in space-time.

CONTINUE ▶

# Reading: Vocab-in-context Questions 1

Donald looked at Tim Capulsky, slumped in front of the television in his hotel room watching the local news. He eyed this man who was his friend, client, and *Line* very possibly the next senator of New Jersey, and was 5 glad to see him inert for a change. It was an exhausting day, and tomorrow wouldn't be much better. Donald had the urge to turn off the TV and carry him to his bed and tuck him in. He chuckled softly at the image and Capulsky turned around but said nothing. Once the 10 program turned from politics to gossip, the candidate stretched and shut the TV off. He looked at his friend.

"Don't worry. I'm happy. May not look it right now, but I'm happy. I'm definitely pleased with all you've been doing. Sometimes I want to tell the folks, 15 'Hey, if you like me, you'll really like the guy whose doing most of the heavy lifting—the brains of the outfit' and then dragging you to the podium."

"Don't do that."

They both smiled almost the exact same smile. An 20 unwelcome rapping at the door broke the moment and Capulsky put a finger to his lips. He made a head-on-pillow gesture and backed his way into his bedroom, saluting his good night. Donald nodded his approval and readied his own excuse as he approached the door.

**MAIN IDEA:** _____

_____

_____ **3.** Which of the following is closest to the meaning of *inert* as it is used in line 5?

**ANTICIPATION:** _____

_____

A) motionless
B) asleep
C) inoperative
D) exhausted

_____ **4.** Which of the following is closest to the meaning of *readied* as it is used in line 24?

**ANTICIPATION:** _____

_____

A) began
B) remembered
C) prepared
D) embellished

CONTINUE

# Reading: Vocab-in-context Questions 2

The state of the art of jazz playing and composition is healthy and productive. The current level of musicianship is impressive: an arresting number of young players today can handle traditional bebop, post-bebop, and more modern, rock-influenced idioms. While some neo-traditionalists such as Wynton Marsalis once called for increased respect for the past and attention to one's craft, such controversies have settled down of late. People feel less inclined to choose sides, and traditionalism sits comfortably with a more forward-thinking, globally-informed sound that nods to the free jazz of the 1960s.

Some believe this means that there is not now, and never again can be, a jazz avant-garde. There is only a safe, innocuous sound and approach that, whatever pleasures it affords and whatever superficial differences exist between performers and pieces, has become so encompassing that nothing will again seem startlingly, brashly, even annoyingly ahead of its time. I suspect that the time is now ripe for just such a phenomenon, but I am less sure that anyone will take advantage of the opportunity.

*Line 5*

*10*

*15*

*20*

**MAIN IDEA:** _____

_____

**_____ 5.** As it is used in line 3, *arresting* most nearly means:

**ANTICIPATION:** _____

_____

A) decreasing
B) impressive
C) halting
D) implausible

**_____ 6.** As it is used in line 15, *innocuous* most nearly means:

**ANTICIPATION:** _____

_____

A) bland
B) painless
C) similar
D) inventive

CONTINUE ➔

# Reading: Main Idea Questions 3

In musical theater, a collection of top-notch songs dwelling within a second-rate story will not last long. Conversely, a compelling drama or truly funny script that comes with some hit-and-miss songs can be a winner. Story, it seems, trumps tune for winning over both audiences and critics. This holds true even for today's "jukebox musicals," shows built around well-loved pop songs. One would think they'd be immune to concerns about story, since the songs are the whole point of the show. Yet, the most successful of these productions are still those in which story delivers the engaging characters, dramatic situations, and few good laughs.

All of which underscores the importance of the "book writer," yet the public still lacks a definite understanding of what these folks do and how they contribute to a show's success. Book writers write the story itself: the plot, setting, dialogue, and anything outside of the music and lyrics. Book writers create the people who inhabit a show. Glorious melodies and clever song lyrics will not much move an audience if put into the mouths of dull or underdeveloped characters. The book writer gives the songwriters the substance to which they can add their art.

*Line 5*

*10*

*15*

*20*

**MAIN IDEA:** _____

_____

**7.** The main idea of the first paragraph is:

**ANTICIPATION:** _____

_____

A) top-notch songs are crucial to the success of a musical.
B) jukebox musicals are the only shows that do not heavily rely on story.
C) no musical without a strong story and top-notch songs is likely to be successful.
D) the quality of the story is more important to a musical's success than that of its songs.

**8.** The main idea of the second paragraph is:

**ANTICIPATION:** _____

_____

A) few people are aware of how important book writers are to jukebox musicals.
B) book writers are unappreciated but crucial to the success of musicals.
C) the music and lyrics to a musical is usually less substantial than the story itself.
D) a musical is unlikely to be successful if the characters in the show are not fully three-dimensional.

**CONTINUE** →

# Math: Algebra

_____ **9.** If $3x + 5 = 17$, $x = ?$

    A) 3
    B) 4
    C) 5
    D) 6

_____ **10.** If $5x - 13 = 32$, $x = ?$

    A) 9
    B) 10
    C) 11
    D) 12

_____ **11.** If $4x - 21 = 56 - 3x$, $x = ?$

    A) 3
    B) 5
    C) 9
    D) 11

_____ **12.** If $\dfrac{3x+8}{2} = 16$, $x = ?$

    A) 5
    B) 6
    C) 7
    D) 8

_____ **13.** If $3(2x - 9) = 15$, $x = ?$

    A) 1
    B) 4
    C) 5
    D) 7

_____ **14.** If $\sqrt{x - 9} = 2$, $x = ?$

    A) −3
    B) 3
    C) 13
    D) 23

_____ **15.** If $(x - 5)(x + 6) = x^2$, $x = ?$

    A) 15
    B) 20
    C) 25
    D) 30

_____ **16.** $4y + 5x + 14 = 2y + 7x + 20$, what is $y$ in terms of $x$?

    A) $y = x - 3$
    B) $y = x + 3$
    C) $y = 2x + 4$
    D) $y = 2x + 6$

$$2a + b = 9$$
$$3b + c = 25$$
$$2a + 3c = 14$$

_____ **17.** Given the system of equations above, what is the value of $a + b + c$?

    A) 8
    B) 10
    C) 12
    D) 16

_____ **18.** If $x + y = 10$ and $x^2 - y^2 = 60$, what is the value of $x - y$?

    A) 6
    B) 8
    C) 10
    D) 12

**STOP**

# Homework 6

## Reading: Double Passage 1

**Passage 1**

Not many Americans today can name one living serious composer (though with a little prodding, they might offer up John Williams, noted creator of the music
*Line* accompanying the Star Wars movies and other
5 blockbusters). People still attend concerts and operas, but the make-up of the audience doesn't bode well for the future of the art. The average age of a typical concertgoer has been on the rise for decades, and attempts to supplant this graying demographic with younger folks
10 has had limited success, especially from an artistic perspective. Putting together a family-friendly program by including popular songs, movie music, etc., does nothing to further the art form that the orchestras and concert halls were created to serve.

**Passage 2**

15 The current condition of concert music in the U.S. might be described as anemic, with a number of factors contributing to its decline. Ticket prices can be prohibitively high, especially the young. Fewer people of any age play instruments—musically literate non-
20 professionals have long made up a sizable portion of regular concertgoers. But the music itself has to take some of the blame as well. The at-times excruciatingly difficult music that became fashionable in the mid-20$^{th}$ century delivered a body blow to concert attendance that
25 is still being felt. But there is reason for optimism. We've seen a resurgence of ear-pleasing but still adventurous music from a growing clutch of youngish composers. Whether the younger folks who enthusiastically attend concerts of this music can spread the word
30 to those in their demographic who never step foot in a concert hall has yet to be determined.

1. Passages 1 and 2 both make the point that:
   A) classical music does not have a sufficiently large audience among young people.
   B) fewer classical music fans today listen to music created by young composers.
   C) the artistic quality of classical music concerts had been on the decline for years.
   D) classical music concerts designed for younger audiences have been unpopular.

2. Unlike the author of Passage 1, the author of Passage 2:
   A) makes the case that attendance at classical music concerts is likely to increase.
   B) criticizes composers from the recent past for writing music that was not adventurous.
   C) points out that people today are less musically knowledgeable.
   D) addresses causes for a decline in interest in classical music.

**MAIN IDEAS:**

A: _____

B: _____

CONTINUE

# Reading: Double Passage 2

### Passage 1

Amid the general concern over climate change, there has been less focus on rainforest deforestation. Deforestation, especially in the Amazon, is of course, a significant driver of global warming: the ldeoss of trees, which consume carbon dioxide, leads to greater amounts of carbon in the air, leading in turn to more heat being trapped in Earth's lower atmosphere.

However, other serious dangers arise from the indiscriminate slash-and-burn approach that continues to be used in the Amazon by loggers and others. The indigenous people have been treated roughly, at times brutally, as their homelands have been destroyed or made uninhabitable. The number of plant and animal species continues to decline at a rate estimated at 50,000 species annually. Deforestation also typically leads to soil erosion, and once fertile areas turn into wasteland.

### Passage 2

A number of steps have been taken to curb the serious environmental dangers associated with defor- estation. One of the most common-sense approaches involves a stricter monitoring of forest loss. Arial photographs can be studied by individuals who do not possess advanced training. Satellite images of so-called hot spots, areas most susceptible to rapid loss, can be analyzed. These methods can be used to track regrowth as well as forest loss.

Another important advance is the development of new farming methods that minimize the amount of deforested land needed by small local farmers by showing them how to increase crop yield. A particularly inventive method for accomplishing this is the creation of food forests that replicate natural forests. These agroforestal systems have proved successful at reducing dependence on fossil fuels and chemicals and improving the quality of the local soil and water. More importantly, this is both a pragmatic and an ethical way to keep in mind the rights of the people who have lived in the forest all their lives.

*Line 5, 10, 15, 20, 25, 30, 35*

3. Both passages mention the people who have always lived in the rainforest, but only Passage 2:

A) involves them in ways to remedy the problem of deforestation.
B) explains how they have helped formulate ways to alleviate the problem of deforestation.
C) states that they have been treated brutally at times in the past.
D) acknowledges that there has been a lessening of habitat loss due to deforestation in recent years.

4. It can be inferred from the passage that the author of Passage 2 would most likely:

A) feel that the author of Passage 1 has overstated the threat posed by deforestation.
B) strongly agree with the concerns expressed by the author of Passage 1.
C) argue that the solutions proposed by the author of Passage 1 are impractical.
D) point out that climate change is only one threat posed by deforestation.

**MAIN IDEAS:**

A: _____

B: _____

CONTINUE

# Reading: Double Passage 3

**Passage 1**

In July of 2011, the General Assembly of the United Nations decided to ask member nations to determine the happiness of their people by simply asking them. The idea *Line* was to see not just how people felt about their lives, but 5 also what aspects of their nations' structure and services added to their happiness or took from it.

The result was the World Happiness Report, which is revised annually. Besides ranking countries based on their World Happiness Index, the report includes analyses of 10 how individual well-being is tied to a nation's progress. Ethics, mental illness, and many other topics are discussed in some depth. Six variables have been identified as being strongly associated with happiness: gross domestic product (GDP) per capita, social support, healthy life 15 expectancy, freedom to make life choices, generosity, and perceived corruption. One country, Bhutan, has gone so far as to make *gross national happiness* its main development indicator.

**Passage 2**

The annual World Happiness Report published by the 20 UN's Sustainable Development Solutions Network is meant to provide insights into how a nation's culture, economy, and governmental structure contributes to its citizens' happiness or, sad to say, their misery. With this knowledge in hand, leaders can then institute policy 25 changes so as to improve lives.

That's the theory anyway. The report has yet to deliver any surprises. As expected, Western European countries, with their well-fed, well-educated, well-protected citizens generally top the charts. Similar 30 countries such as New Zealand and the U.S. also score well, usually in the top 15 out of more than 150 countries. This is not terribly useful information to poorer countries who strive for greater happiness.

**MAIN IDEAS:**

A: _____

B: _____

5. The author of Passage 2, unlike the author of Passage 1, uses a tone that is sometimes

A) optimistic
B) humorous
C) skeptical
D) morose

6. Which of the following best describes a difference between the two passages?

A) Passage 1 focuses on the content of the report, while Passage 2 focuses on the purpose of the report.
B) Passage 1 focuses on the results of the report, while Passage 2 focuses on the format of the report.
C) Passage 1 focuses on changes to the report since its inception, while Passage 2 focuses on the report's creation.
D) Passage 1 provides data about individual nations that took part in the index, while Passage 2 provides data regarding the ranking of the nations in the index.

CONTINUE

# Math: Function Notation

**Questions 7 to 12 refer to the following function:**

> Let $h(x) = x^2 + 3x$

_____ **7.** $h(2) = ?$

    A)    5
    B)    7
    C)    10
    D)    12

_____ **8.** $h(3) = ?$

    A)    6
    B)    9
    C)    12
    D)    18

_____ **9.** $h(-2) = ?$

    A)    -10
    B)    -2
    C)    -1
    D)    10

_____ **10.** $h(7) = ?$

    A)    28
    B)    49
    C)    52
    D)    70

_____ **11.** $h(0) = ?$

    A)    -3
    B)    0
    C)    3
    D)    9

_____ **12.** If $h(k) = 0$, which of the following could be the value of $k$?

    A)    -3
    B)    -1
    C)    3
    D)    9

**Questions 13 to 16 refer to the following function:**

> Let $f(x) = (x - 3)^2$
> Let $g(x) = 2x - 1$

_____ **13.** $f(5) = ?$

    A)    2
    B)    4
    C)    8
    D)    16

_____ **14.** $f(12) = ?$

    A)    9
    B)    18
    C)    27
    D)    81

_____ **15.** $g(8) = ?$

    A)    15
    B)    17
    C)    19
    D)    23

_____ **16.** If $g(4) = a$, what is $f(a)$ ?

    A)    1
    B)    7
    C)    15
    D)    16

CONTINUE ➤

# Math: FOIL

_____ **17.** $(x + 3)(x + 2) = ?$

    A) $x^2 + x + 5$
    B) $x^2 + 5x + 5$
    C) $x^2 + 5x + 6$
    D) $x^2 + 6x + 5$

_____ **18.** $(x + 4)(x - 1) = ?$

    A) $x^2 + 3x - 4$
    B) $x^2 + 3x + 3$
    C) $x^2 + 5x - 4$
    D) $x^2 - 3x - 4$

_____ **19.** $(x - 5)(x - 6) = ?$

    A) $x^2 - x - 11$
    B) $x^2 - x - 30$
    C) $x^2 + 11x + 30$
    D) $x^2 - 11x + 30$

_____ **20.** $(x - 2)(x + 1) = ?$

    A) $x^2 + x - 2$
    B) $x^2 - x + 2$
    C) $x^2 - x - 2$
    D) $x^2 - 2x - 2$

_____ **21.** $(2x - 1)(x + 3) = ?$

    A) $2x^2 + 2x - 3$
    B) $2x^2 + 5x - 3$
    C) $2x^2 + 6x - 3$
    D) $2x^2 + 7x + 3$

_____ **22.** $(3x + 5)(4x - 2) = ?$

    A) $7x^2 + 3x - 10$
    B) $7x^2 + 14x - 10$
    C) $12x^2 + 7x + 10$
    D) $12x^2 + 14x - 10$

_____ **23.** $(2x - 3)(7x - 4) = ?$

    A) $9x^2 - 7x + 12$
    B) $9x^2 - 13x - 1$
    C) $14x^2 - 29x - 12$
    D) $14x^2 - 29x + 12$

_____ **24.** $(10x + 3)(5x + 12) = ?$

    A) $15x^2 + 135x + 36$
    B) $15x^2 + 150x + 15$
    C) $50x^2 + 135x + 36$
    D) $50x^2 + 150x + 120$

_____ **25.** $(5x - 1)(-3x + 8) = ?$

    A) $-15x^2 + 43x - 8$
    B) $-15x^2 - 37x - 8$
    C) $15x^2 - 43x + 8$
    D) $15x^2 + 37x - 8$

_____ **26.** $(-2x + 9)(-4x + 10) = ?$

    A) $-8x^2 - 56x + 90$
    B) $-8x^2 - 36x - 20$
    C) $8x^2 - 56x + 90$
    D) $8x^2 - 36x + 90$

**STOP**

# Homework 7

## Writing: Commas 1

_____ 1. As the lead scientist on the university's new nanobot research <u>team, Dr. Neilson</u> found she spent more time managing the other researchers than doing experiments herself.

1. A) NO CHANGE
   B) team Dr. Neilson,
   C) team, Dr. Neilson,
   D) team; Dr. Neilson

_____ 2. King Leopold II of <u>Belgium, founded a brutally exploitative</u> "Free State" in the Congo by convincing other Europeans that he was engaged in humanitarian work.

2. A) NO CHANGE
   B) Belgium founded, a brutally exploitative
   C) Belgium founded a brutally exploitative
   D) Belgium, founded a brutally exploitative,

_____ 3. John Carpenter's gruesome horror <u>movie *The Thing* made in 1982,</u> is often considered the apex of achievement in practical special effects.

3. A) NO CHANGE
   B) movie *The Thing* made in 1982
   C) movie, *The Thing* made in 1982
   D) movie *The Thing*, made in 1982,

_____ 4. Anybody who knew Stella could tell <u>you that she loved,</u> her dog, her music, and her beat-up pickup truck.

4. A) NO CHANGE
   B) you that, she loved
   C) you, that she loved,
   D) you that she loved

_____ 5. The ascension of Maria Theresa to the throne of <u>Austria, led directly to the War of Austrian Succession,</u> which lasted almost eight years and embroiled most of Europe's great powers.

5. A) NO CHANGE
   B) Austria led directly to the War of Austrian Succession,
   C) Austria led directly, to the War of Austrian Succession
   D) Austria, led directly to the War of Austrian Succession

CONTINUE ➡

# Writing: Commas 2

_____ **6.** Andy always preferred to go to the <u>beach, on the north side</u> of the harbor because it was usually less crowded.

**6.** A) NO CHANGE
B) beach on the north side,
C) beach, on the north side,
D) beach on the north side

_____ **7.** Capable of reaching speeds over two hundred miles per <u>hour, the peregrine falcon is the fastest animal on Earth,</u> an honor many mistakenly bestow on the cheetah.

**7.** A) NO CHANGE
B) hour the peregrine falcon is the fastest animal on Earth,
C) hour the peregrine falcon is the fastest animal on Earth
D) hour, the peregrine falcon, is the fastest animal on Earth

_____ **8.** Many of my friends believe that the old mental <u>hospital an abandoned building, across the street, from our school</u> is haunted.

**8.** A) NO CHANGE
B) hospital, an abandoned building across the street from our school,
C) hospital, an abandoned building across the street, from our school
D) hospital an abandoned building, across the street, from our school,

_____ **9.** Melissa's grandfather was a renowned crime-scene <u>photographer, in Chicago, and,</u> she has decorated her apartment with dozens of his most interesting works.

**9.** A) NO CHANGE
B) photographer, in Chicago and
C) photographer in Chicago, and
D) photographer in, Chicago and

_____ **10.** Before he created <u>Mario possibly the most famous video game character of all time,</u> Shigeru Miyamoto was employed by Nintendo to create artwork that would adorn arcade machines.

**10.** A) NO CHANGE
B) Mario, possibly the most famous video game character of all time,
C) Mario, possibly, the most famous video game character of all time
D) Mario, possibly the most famous video game character, of all time

CONTINUE →

# Writing: Apostrophes 1

_____ 11. The unfortunate nexus of air <u>current's in the office meant Yvonne's</u> desk was always freezing when the air conditioning was active.

11. A) NO CHANGE
   B) current's in the office meant Yvonnes
   C) currents' in the office meant Yvonnes
   D) currents in the office meant Yvonne's

_____ 12. By design, it's difficult to determine where this <u>sentences' apostrophes</u> should be placed.

12. A) NO CHANGE
   B) sentence's apostrophes
   C) sentences apostrophes'
   D) sentence's apostrophe's

_____ 13. The <u>scientists' noses'</u> all wrinkled in unison when confronted with the ghastly results of their attempt to design a new deodorant.

13. A) NO CHANGE
   B) scientists nose's
   C) scientists' noses
   D) scientist's noses

_____ 14. In the raffle, Taylor won a <u>series of cooking lessons from the restaurant's</u> gregarious head chef.

14. A) NO CHANGE
   B) series of cooking lessons' from the restaurant's
   C) series' of cooking lessons from the restaurants
   D) series of cooking lesson's from the restaurants

_____ 15. The <u>neighborhoods criminal elements</u> don't stand a chance against its newest hero!

15. A) NO CHANGE
   B) neighborhoods' criminal elements
   C) neighborhood's criminal elements
   D) neighborhoods criminal elements'

CONTINUE

# Writing: Other Punctuation 1

_____ **16.** My friend Naomi—a pediatric surgeon at the local children's <u>hospital,</u> is one of the hardest-working people I know.

**16.**
A) NO CHANGE
B) hospital
C) hospital;
D) hospital—

_____ **17.** Simon Bolivar dreamed of a unified and democratic South <u>America, however,</u> in the years immediately after his death, foreign intervention and political infighting quickly dissolved that dream.

**17/**
A) NO CHANGE
B) America however;
C) America; however,
D) America, however—

_____ **18.** Before the invention of printing <u>press, creating</u> a new book involved hundreds of hours of meticulous copying by hand, often done by monks.

**18.**
A) NO CHANGE
B) press. Creating
C) press: creating
D) press; creating

_____ **19.** Despite the dramatically increasing cost of rent, having increased by more than fifty percent over the last five <u>years—</u>people continue to move to New York City at record rates.

**19.**
A) NO CHANGE
B) years,
C) years;
D) years:

_____ **20.** Building new subway lines can be expensive <u>business, if we want to increase capacity and remain in the black,</u> we should focus on refining the service on our existing infrastructure.

**20.**
A) NO CHANGE
B) business; if we want to increase capacity and remain in the black;
C) business; if we want to increase capacity and remain in the black,
D) business if we want to increase capacity and remain in the black,

CONTINUE ➡

# Math: Factoring

**21.** The expression $(3x - 2)(5x + 8)$ is equivalent to:

- A) $15x^2 - 14x - 16$
- B) $15x^2 + 14x - 16$
- C) $15x^2 - 14x + 16$
- D) $15x^2 - 16$

**22.** Which of the following expressions is equivalent to $10x^2 + 25x + 15$ ?

- A) $(x + 10)(x + 15)$
- B) $(x - 1)(10x + 15)$
- C) $(x + 1)(10x + 15)$
- D) $(x - 1)(15x - 10)$

**23.** Which of the following expressions is equivalent to: $16x^2 + 8x + 1 = 0$ ?

- A) $(4x + 1)^2$
- B) $(4x + 1)(4x - 1)$
- C) $(4x - 1)^2$
- D) $(1 - 4x)^2$

**24.** Which of the following expressions is a factored form of $6xy^5 + 3x^5y$ ?

- A) $6x^4y^4$
- B) $6xy(y^4 + x^4)$
- C) $3xy(2y^4 + x^4)$
- D) $3x^4y^4(2y + x)$

**25.** Which of the following choices shows all of the positive factors of the number 16?

- A) 1, 2, 4, 8, 16
- B) 1, 2, 4, 16
- C) 1, 2, 4, 12, 32
- D) 1, 8, 16, 32

**26.** Which of the following expressions is equivalent to $(x + 3)(x^2 + 3x - 5)$ ?

- A) $x^3 + 6x^2 + 4x - 15$
- B) $x^3 + 3x^2 + 12x - 15$
- C) $x^3 + 3x^2 + 9x - 15$
- D) $x^3 + 6x^2 + 2x - 15$

**27.** Which of the following expressions is equivalent to $6x^2 + 5x - 6$ ?

- A) $(3x - 2)(3x + 3)$
- B) $(3 - 2x)(2 - 3x)$
- C) $(2x - 3)(3x + 2)$
- D) $(2x + 3)(3x - 2)$

**28.** Which of the following expressions is equivalent to $x^2 - 25$ ?

- A) $(x + 5)(x + 5)$
- B) $(x + 5)(x - 5)$
- C) $(x + 5)^2$
- D) $(x - 5)^2$

**29.** The expression given below is equivalent to which of the following expressions $8x^2 - 22x - 21$ ?

- A) $(2x + 7)(4x - 3)$
- B) $(2x - 7)(4x + 3)$
- C) $(7x + 2)(3x - 4)$
- D) $(7x - 2)(3x + 4)$

**30.** Which of the following choices shows all of the positive factors of the number 18?

- A) 1, 3, 4, 6, 9, 18
- B) 1, 3, 6, 9, 12
- C) 1, 2, 6, 9, 36
- D) 1, 2, 3, 6, 9, 18

**STOP**

# Homework 8

## Writing: Redundancy 1

_____ 1. <u>Every year, our</u> glee club's annual charity benefit raises money to fund music education in poor countries around the world.

1. A) NO CHANGE
   B) Once a year, our
   C) Our
   D) As a yearly charity event, our

_____ 2. Last year my family took a trip to the Netherlands, and I was amazed by the clean public <u>parks there that were so neat.</u>

2. A) NO CHANGE
   B) parks there in the Netherlands.
   C) tidily there in the Netherlands.
   D) parks.

_____ 3. Owen and Logan are pooling their money to buy an advanced digital camera, so they can film the movie script that <u>Owen wrote.</u>

3. A) NO CHANGE
   B) he wrote.
   C) Owen wrote for a movie.
   D) was written by him for them to film.

_____ 4. Isabel knew that she shouldn't open the <u>strange, rumbling box that was making noise</u> in the corner of her grandparent's attic.

4. A) NO CHANGE
   B) odd, rumbling box that was strange
   C) strange, rumbling box
   D) odd and strange box

_____ 5. Pyramids can be found around the world. They were often built by slaves and usually served as religious <u>buildings across the globe.</u>

5. A) NO CHANGE
   B) buildings globally.
   C) buildings.
   D) structures anywhere in the world.

CONTINUE ➡

# Writing: Redundancy 2

_____ 6. Stringed instruments played by hand have existed for thousands of years, but the first instruments with recognizable similarities to modern guitars were created in Spain in the 13th century. They have traits in common with modern guitars.

6. A) NO CHANGE
   B) These Spanish instruments share a number of traits with modern guitars.
   C) Modern guitars have a number of similarities to them.
   D) DELETE the underlined portion.

_____ 7. Because his car broke down, all week my friend has found himself in the unfortunate and luckless position of needing to ask his older brother for a ride to work.

7. A) NO CHANGE
   B) unfortunate position
   C) unlucky position for the whole week
   D) lucklessly unfortunate position

_____ 8. Our local tennis club, which serves the nearby area, is planning a tournament for Labor Day weekend.

8. A) NO CHANGE
   B) club
   C) club of tennis players
   D) club, which plays tennis,

_____ 9. Victoria eased past the old marble statue and carefully avoided touching its marble form with great care to prevent it from collapsing.

9. A) NO CHANGE
   B) with great care avoided touching or contacting it
   C) carefully avoided touching it
   D) using great care avoided any contact so as not to touch the statue

_____ 10. Sierra was very proud of her encyclopedic knowledge of mid-nineties television shows and was happy to demonstrate it at parties.

10. A) NO CHANGE
    B) happy and amicable
    C) happy to show and
    D) DELETE the underlined portion.

CONTINUE

# Writing: Transitions 1

_____ 11. Robert the Bald defeated Prince Ethelrood at the Battle of the Three Rivers. He was, <u>however,</u> able to the prince's throne by right of conquest.

11. A) NO CHANGE
    B) nevertheless,
    C) therefore,
    D) previously,

_____ 12. When it comes to running the restaurant, my boss micromanages us way too much. <u>Nevertheless,</u> he makes us account for where every lemon slice goes, and he refuses to let anyone else fold the napkins.

12. A) NO CHANGE
    B) On the other hand,
    C) For example,
    D) Surprisingly,

_____ 13. The Brontë sisters—Charlotte, Emily, and Anne—may very well make up the most talented family of writers in human history. <u>All three</u> enjoyed success as poets and novelists.

13. A) NO CHANGE
    B) However, all three
    C) All three, in contrast,
    D) Therefore, all three

_____ 14. <u>Because</u> the Berlin Wall was brought down more than 25 years ago, differences between the two halves of the city remain.

14. A) NO CHANGE
    B) Although
    C) Before
    D) If

_____ 15. The research team believes there may be a link between low rainfall and the migration routes of geese. <u>For example,</u> they will tag several specimens to track whether the geese appear in areas that have recently experienced drought.

15. A) NO CHANGE
    B) Nevertheless,
    C) Coincidentally,
    D) For this reason,

**CONTINUE** ➡

# Writing: Transitions 2

_____ **16.** To celebrate the 4th of July, the city council has planned a giant parade and a million-dollar fireworks spectacle. The whole plan may be in jeopardy, additionally, if this torrential rain refuses to stop.

**16.** A) NO CHANGE
B) therefore,
C) for instance,
D) however,

_____ **17.** Because there is disagreement about what level of soccer counts as "professional", it is difficult to determine the leading scorer of all time. Conversely, some sources name Pelé as having the most goals while others believe it to be Josef Bican.

**17.** A) NO CHANGE
B) On the other hand,
C) Consequently,
D) At that time,

_____ **18.** *Turritopsis dohrnii* is a species of jellyfish that is able to revert from its adult state back to an immature polyp at any time. In light of this ability, the species is called the "immortal jellyfish."

**18.** A) NO CHANGE
B) Despite this talent,
C) That is because
D) Surprisingly, this means

_____ **19.** Theories about the true authorship of Shakespeare's plays are plentiful. In the academic community, therefore, proposed alternative authors are rarely taken seriously, as there is no concrete evidence to suggest any of them wrote the plays.

**19.** A) NO CHANGE
B) as one example,
C) similarly,
D) however,

_____ **20.** At the annual harvest festival, the villagers would bring all their crops to the square to be judged, while those chosen as the finest would be brought to the temple at the top of the mountain.

**20.** A) NO CHANGE
B) although
C) during which
D) after which

CONTINUE

# Math: Graphing Functions

_____ **21.** What is the slope of the line that passes through the points $(1, 2)$ and $(3, 8)$ ?

A) $-3$
B) $-1/3$
C) $1/3$
D) $3$

_____ **22.** What is the slope of the line that passes through the points $(-6, 4)$ and $(1, -3)$ ?

A) $-7/6$
B) $-6/7$
C) $-1$
D) $1$

_____ **23.** What is the $y$-intercept of the line that passes through the points $(1, -1)$ and $(5, 7)$ ?

A) $-3$
B) $-2$
C) $-1$
D) $1$

_____ **24.** What is the $x$-intercept of the line that passes through the points $(1, -1)$ and $(5, 7)$ ?

A) $1/2$
B) $3/2$
C) $5/2$
D) $7/2$

_____ **25.** The equation of line $\ell$ is $y = 3x + 7$. If line $k$ is perpendicular to line $\ell$, what is the slope of line $k$?

A) $-3$
B) $-1/3$
C) $1/3$
D) $3/7$

_____ **26.** The equation of line $\ell$ is $y = 3x - 1$. If line $m$ is the reflection of line $\ell$ across the $x$-axis, what is the slope of line $m$?

A) $-3$
B) $-1/3$
C) $-1$
D) $1/3$

_____ **27.** The equation of line $\ell$ is $y = -2x + 3$. If line $k$ is parallel to line $\ell$ and passes through the point $(3,5)$, what is the $y$-intercept of line $k$?

A) $8$
B) $9$
C) $10$
D) $11$

CONTINUE

_____ **28.** Which of the following could be the graph of

$$y = -\frac{1}{2}x + 2 ?$$

A)

B)

C)

D)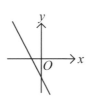

_____ **30.** Let the function $f$ be defined by

$$f(x) = ax^2 + bx + c$$ where $a$, $b$, and $c$ are constants. If $a < 0$ and $c > 0$, then which of the following could be the graph of $f$?

A)

B)

C)

D)

_____ **29.** Which of the following could be the graph of
$y = 2x - 3 ?$

A)

B)

C)

D)

**STOP**

# Course B

2 hr 30 hr

# Homework 1

## Reading: Main Idea Questions 1

Vegetarianism in on the rise in virtually all demographic groups in the United States and in much of the rest of the world. Even more impressive is the rate

*Line*
5
of increase in the percentage of the U.S. population that has substantially cut back on their animal product intake. These changes are not fads: analysts of every segment of the food industry agree that the American diet has irrevocably altered.

The reasons for this are many and overlapping.
10 Nutrition and animal well-being, not surprisingly, are the most often cited, but increasingly, recent converts to vegetarianism mention cost, weight loss, food safety, and religious proscriptions as motivating factors. Interestingly, the reason most often given by *non-*
15 *vegetarians* for why they choose to remain meat-eaters—taste—also plays a role in the decision of others to forego animal products. In the last ten years, food manufacturers have become more skilled at producing easy-to-prepare vegetarian items that simply taste
20 delicious.

**MAIN IDEA:** _____

_____

_____ 1. The primary function of the first paragraph is to:

**ANTICIPATION:** _____

_____

A) briefly describe the how the food industry tracks vegetarianism.
B) explain that the United States has started a worldwide rise in vegetarianism.
C) show that the author approves in the rise in vegetarianism.
D) identify the trend that people in the United States eat less meat and will continue to do so.

_____ 2. The main purpose of the second paragraph is to:

**ANTICIPATION:** _____

_____

A) give arguments in favor of the changes discussed in the first paragraph.
B) present an overview of a range of recent changes that have taken place in the American diet.
C) discuss changes in the manufacturing process of vegetarian meals.
D) provide possible explanations for the increase in vegetarianism.

CONTINUE

# Reading: Main Idea Questions 2

A recent nationwide poll confirms what one hears daily from news media of every stripe: most Americans believe that the country is more polarized than at any time in recent history. Specifically, 81% of respondents said the country "definitely" or "almost certainly" more divided by social and political issues than it has been since the Civil War. Similarly, 89% agreed that political discourse has become more antagonistic in the last 50 years.

*Line 5*

While these results are clear enough, the question remains: are they right? Are we really that divided? The attempt to determine how well this appraisal reflects actual state of affairs has been elusive. This same survey found that while most people describing themselves as "politically conservative" agreed about the general meaning of that phrase, they were not nearly as much in agreement about specific policy issues. Even those who self-described as "very conservative" or "very liberal" shared significant views on a number of relevant issues. Measuring levels of antagonism is similarly difficult. Does one measure presidential vetoes or perhaps overturns of vetoes? The number of protests? Instances of violence?

*10*

*15*

*20*

**MAIN IDEA:** _____

_____

_____ 3. What is the main idea of the first paragraph?

**ANTICIPATION:** _____

_____

A) The country is not nearly as divided as most people believe it to be.
B) Evidence shows a large majority of people believe the country is politically divided.
C) The news media has correctly predicted the attitudes of most Americans.
D) America has been becoming steadily more divided since the Civil War.

_____ 4. What is the main idea of the second paragraph?

**ANTICIPATION:** _____

_____

A) Most people in the United States have more in common with each other than they realize.
B) Respondents did not correctly understand the meanings of the words they used to describe themselves.
C) Though the level of polarization in the United States is considerable, the apparent level of antagonism is overstated.
D) It is difficult to determine whether the country is really as polarized as people believe it to be.

CONTINUE ▶

# Math: Plug In

**DIRECTIONS: You must use Plug In** on each of the following questions. Write your answer in the space before the question number.

_____ **5.** Alan has $x$ chocolate bars and gets 10 more bars. He gives away half of his chocolate, and then gets another 10 bars. In terms of $x$, how many chocolate bars does Alan now have?

A) $x + 15$
B) $x + 20$
C) $\dfrac{x}{2}$
D) $\dfrac{x}{2} + 15$

_____ **6.** If $a$ is 5 less than twice $b$, which of the following gives $b$ in terms of $a$?

A) $2a - 5$
B) $5 + 2a$
C) $\dfrac{5 - a}{2}$
D) $\dfrac{a + 5}{2}$

_____ **7.** Stewart's car can hold a maximum of $g$ gallons in its gas tank, and gas costs $c$ dollars per gallon. If the car currently has 2 gallons of gas in the tank, what is the cost, in dollars, to fill up the rest of the tank?

A) $cg - 2$
B) $cg - 2c$
C) $cg - 2g$
D) $g - 2c$

_____ **8.** In a series of three numbers, the second number is 3 less than the first, and the third is three times the second. If the first number is $x$, how much greater than the second number is the third number?

A) $2x - 6$
B) $2x - 9$
C) $2x - 12$
D) $3x - 3$

_____ **9.** Olivia earns a commission of 15 percent of the price of every boat she sells. Which of the following gives the amount of her commission, in dollars, if she sells $x$ boats that each cost $y$ dollars?

A) $15xy$
B) $1500xy$
C) $\dfrac{3xy}{20}$
D) $\dfrac{3y}{20x}$

**STOP**

# Homework 2

## Reading: Passage 1

Most people use the word "hobo" as little more than a derogatory term for the homeless, deriding them as lazy bums who spend their days idly wandering the
*Line* country. However, the word properly refers to an
5   itinerant worker. Far from lazy, hobos travel hundreds of miles looking for any work they can find. When jobs were especially scarce during the Great Depression several hundred thousand hobos traveled from town to town, hitching rides in railway freight cars and carrying
10  only the bare essentials on their backs. As their numbers increased, hobo culture became more organized, developing ways to communicate with each other to keep safe. These included homemade travel books and a system of written symbols to inform other hobos
15  whether nearby houses were friendly or hostile. Today, hobos even have their own union and an annual convention in Britt, Iowa, home of the National Hobo Museum.

**MAIN IDEA:** _____

_____

_____ **1.** In context, the author includes lines 1-4 ("Most... country") in order to

**ANTICIPATION:** _____

_____

A) present a common opinion the author will refute
B) demonstrate the proper connotation of a word
C) disparage the indolence of the hobo lifestyle
D) detail the history of itinerant workers in the U.S.

_____ **2.** The "books" (line 13) and the "system" (line 14) are given as examples of

**ANTICIPATION:** _____

_____

A) objects that can be seen in the National Hobo Museum
B) the dangers that hobos can encounter on the road
C) methods hobos use for interacting with their peers
D) tools needed to perform a typical job that a hobo finds

CONTINUE ➤

# Reading: Passage 2

Americans are spoiled by the mutual intelligibility of the regional variations of their language. The differences between dialects within the country are
*Line* trivial, such as whether a carbonated beverage is called
5 "soda" or "pop" or whether "caramel" should be pronounced with two syllables or three. When compared with other languages, American English shows astonishing little variation. In Germany, for example, there are over a dozen distinct Germanic languages
10 spoken, from Alemannic to Westphalian, some of which have deep grammatical differences beyond simple vocabulary or phonology. The difference can be starker with German spoken in other countries: the "German" spoken in Switzerland is practically incomprehensible to
15 one who speaks only Standard German. When Americans travel in America, other people may sound funny, but they understand each other. If a German strays too far from home, the people around him might as well be speaking Latin.

**MAIN IDEA:** _____

_____

_____ **3.** The author says Americans are "spoiled" (line 1) because they

**ANTICIPATION:** _____

_____

A) struggle to learn many different varieties of American English
B) use different words for common things than people from other parts of the country
C) have little difficulty understanding each other compared with people in other countries
D) speak a language that has no variation across the country

_____ **4.** In line 19, "Latin" serves as an example of a language that

**ANTICIPATION:** _____

_____

A) has significant dialectical variation
B) is a dialect spoken within Germany
C) only varies in simple vocabulary and phonology
D) is so foreign that it is incomprehensible

CONTINUE ➤

# Reading: Passage 3

George Balanchine is rightly remembered as one of the greatest choreographers of our time, but his muses, the women who inspired him, are just as deserving of
*Line* acclaim. He seemingly was never without a muse, from
5 Vera Zorina in Broadway musicals and Hollywood films, to prima ballerina Maria Tallchief in *The Nutcracker* and *Swan Lake*, to Suzanne Farrell in *Meditation* and *Don Quixote*. These women did not simply perform his work: the work itself would not exist
10 without them. Unlike a painter or a writer, a choreographer like Balanchine is only one of many contributors to an artwork, and his muses can actively shape the result. The dancers are directed by his designs, but his designs are also transformed by their dancing.
15 Each of Balanchine's works merged his artistic vision with a different dancer's soul and spirit.

**MAIN IDEA:** _____

_____

**_____ 5.** The author of the passage argues that Balanchine's "muses" (line 2)

**ANTICIPATION:** _____

_____

A) believed they did not get recognition for their contributions
B) deserve more credit than Balanchine for the value of his work
C) significantly contributed to Balanchine's work
D) were not sufficiently appreciated by Balanchine

**_____ 6.** In lines 10-13 ("Unlike … the result") the author suggests

**ANTICIPATION:** _____

_____

A) painters and writers do not generally have muses
B) Balanchine was unhappy about his lack of control over his work
C) female painters and writers have fewer opportunities than female dancers
D) some artists have greater effect on their own work than Balanchine had

CONTINUE

# Math: Backsolve

**DIRECTIONS: You must use Backsolve** on each of the following questions. Write your answer in the space before the question number.

_____ 7. Tree X is 23 inches tall and tree Y is 73 inches tall. Tree X grows 5 inches a year and tree Y grows 3 inches a year. In how many years will tree X be the same height as tree Y?

A) 10
B) 15
C) 25
D) 30

$$a + b = 17$$
$$b + c = 35$$
$$a + c = 28$$

_____ 10. In the system of equations above, what is the value of $a$?

A) 5
B) 10
C) 12
D) 24

_____ 8. At a movie theater, small drinks cost $3 each and large drinks cost $5 each. The theater sells 100 total drinks for a total of $380. How many small drinks were sold?

A) 45
B) 50
C) 55
D) 60

_____ 11. Molly has 36 more red shirts than blue shirts. Half the number of red shirts equals twice the number of blue shirts. How many blue shirts does she have?

A) 9
B) 12
C) 24
D) 36

$$B(d) = 2d^2 + 10$$

_____ 9. The function $B$, defined above, models the number of new bees born in a beehive after $d$ days. According to this model, how many days would it take for the colony to gain 108 new bees?

A) 4
B) 5
C) 6
D) 7

**STOP**

# Homework 3

## Writing: Verbs 1

_____ 1. My best friend, who enjoys making music and plays several instruments, <u>plan</u> to visit Maine this winter and write songs in a cabin.

1. A) NO CHANGE
   B) have planned
   C) are planning
   D) plans

_____ 2. When they worked together at the library, Naomi and Nicholas <u>hunt</u> through the aisles for books with ridiculous names.

2. A) NO CHANGE
   B) will hunt
   C) would hunt
   D) are hunting

_____ 3. It looks like our hike might be cut short because a swarm of angry bees <u>have blocked</u> the trail ahead.

3. A) NO CHANGE
   B) is blocking
   C) would block
   D) are blocking

_____ 4. In 1965, Soviet cosmonaut Alexey Leonov <u>will perform</u> the first extra-vehicular space walk in human history.

4. A) NO CHANGE
   B) performs
   C) performed
   D) has performed

_____ 5. The dulcet tones of the piano that had been drifting across the restaurant to the table where Danny waited for his date <u>were</u> suddenly drowned out by the sound of a blender running in the kitchen.

5. A) NO CHANGE
   B) has been
   C) was
   D) is

CONTINUE ➜

# Writing: Verbs 2

_____ 6. In Professor Tomlin's lab, a team of undergraduate students <u>have found</u> a way to "listen" to space by monitoring radio waves as they travel through the cosmic void.

6. A) NO CHANGE
   B) are finding
   C) find
   D) has found

_____ 7. Past the stone monument that marks the end of the beach, <u>lies</u> two tide pools that glitter beautifully in the moonlight.

7. A) NO CHANGE
   B) lie
   C) has lied
   D) is

_____ 8. Next spring, the Emergency Response Team created by the previous mayor <u>has been</u> replaced by a smaller Emergency Dispatch Service that will direct existing resources to respond to crises.

8. A) NO CHANGE
   B) was
   C) is
   D) will be

_____ 9. The requests that Joanna's employees made— on a number of topics but most notably for more vacation time—<u>were</u> reasonable, so she happily changed her policies.

9. A) NO CHANGE
   B) would be
   C) was
   D) is

_____ 10. Because it <u>had been containing</u> private details about his own life and family, Eugene O'Neill's masterpiece *A Long Day's Journey Into Night* was not published until after his death.

10. A) NO CHANGE
    B) contained
    C) will contain
    D) has contained

CONTINUE ➤

# Writing: Verbs 3

_____ **11.** Although Katrina originally learned to code so that she could make video games, now she <u>used</u> those skills to make websites and design phone apps.

**11.** A) NO CHANGE
B) had used
C) uses
D) would use

_____ **12.** The Wonder Wheel and the House of Horror, both of which are over sixty years old, <u>are</u> the most popular rides on the Boardwalk since they first appeared.

**12.** A) NO CHANGE
B) is
C) was
D) have been

_____ **13.** Marco Polo <u>transcribed</u> the famous story of his voyage around the world while he was a prisoner of war in Genoa.

**13.** A) NO CHANGE
B) transcribes
C) has transcribed
D) is transcribing

_____ **14.** Kobe's collection of snakes, seahorses, and storks <u>have been</u> called both unusual and dangerous.

**14.** A) NO CHANGE
B) are
C) has been
D) were

_____ **15.** The herd of sheep in Maria's fields <u>were</u> so large that it was impossible count; all she knew was that she had more than three thousand.

**15.** A) NO CHANGE
B) are
C) was
D) is

**CONTINUE**

# Math: Fundamentals Review

_____ **16.** If $\dfrac{a}{2} \times \dfrac{1}{8} = \dfrac{\frac{3}{4}}{6}$ , then $a = ?$

   A)  2
   B)  3
   C)  4
   D)  6

_____ **17.** What is the remainder when 52 is divided by 3?

   A)  0
   B)  1
   C)  2
   D)  3

_____ **18.** A recipe calls for 3 cups of flour for every 5 cups of sugar. If Bill uses 15 cups of flour, how many cups of sugar should he use?

   A)  10
   B)  15
   C)  20
   D)  25

_____ **19.** A certain park contains only maple and elm trees in a ratio of 2 to 3, respectively. If there are a total of 40 trees, how many elm trees are there in the park?

   A)  16
   B)  18
   C)  20
   D)  24

_____ **20.** What percent of 40 is 8?

   A)  5
   B)  10
   C)  20
   D)  30

_____ **21.** 9 is 15 percent of what number?

   A)  60
   B)  70
   C)  75
   D)  80

_____ **22.** Joe made 160 dollars last week and 180 dollars this week. What was the percent increase in his pay?

   A)  10
   B)  12.5
   C)  15
   D)  17.5

_____ **23.** $x^3\left(x^2\right)^5 = ?$

   A)  $x^5$
   B)  $x^7$
   C)  $x^{10}$
   D)  $x^{13}$

_____ **24.** If $d^3 \times d^4 = d^p$ and $\dfrac{d^{12}}{d^6} = d^q$ , what is $p + q$ ?

   A)  1
   B)  6
   C)  7
   D)  13

_____ **25.** If $|x - 6| = 23$, which of the following gives all possible values of $x$?

   A)  $-29$
   B)  $-17$
   C)  $-17$ and $29$
   D)  $17$ and $-29$

**STOP**

# Homework 4

## Writing: Pronouns 1

_____ 1. All the apartments in the new buildings have a new washing machine for the convenience of <u>it's</u> occupants.

1. A) NO CHANGE
   B) their
   C) its
   D) there

_____ 2. I thought this coat looked great on me at the store, but when I got home I found that <u>it's</u> not exactly the color I expected.

2. A) NO CHANGE
   B) its
   C) its'
   D) they're

_____ 3. Ian loved the look of his new phone, but disliked <u>its'</u> lack of features.

3. A) NO CHANGE
   B) their
   C) its
   D) it's

_____ 4. Every meeting of the Iowa Misanthrope Club ends with a vote for a new chairperson, <u>whom</u> would be forced to host the next meeting.

4. A) NO CHANGE
   B) who
   C) which
   D) whose

_____ 5. If one wishes to build a successful business, <u>they</u> should carefully consider how to stand out from competing ventures.

5. A) NO CHANGE
   B) we
   C) you
   D) one

CONTINUE

# Writing: Pronouns 2

_____ **6.** The school's new policy allows students to easily obtain a copy of <u>their</u> attendance or academic records at any point during the year.

**6.** A) NO CHANGE
B) his or her
C) they're
D) your

_____ **7.** Paul and Olivia liked how <u>they're</u> new back yard opened up directly to a meadow with a tiny stream.

**7.** A) NO CHANGE
B) its
C) there
D) their

_____ **8.** The hippopotamus, despite having an innocuous appearance, is actually extremely dangerous and can kill with <u>their</u> powerful bite.

**8.** A) NO CHANGE
B) they're
C) its
D) it's

_____ **9.** Scientists at NASA are planning a mission to bring an asteroid into lunar orbit so <u>they</u> can be studied more easily by astronauts.

**9.** A) NO CHANGE
B) it
C) which
D) them

_____ **10.** After the conclusion of the piano recital, the teacher asked <u>my friend and I</u> to play a duet together as the audience left the auditorium.

**10.** A) NO CHANGE
B) my friend and me
C) I and my friend
D) my friend and myself

# Writing: Pronouns 3

_____ 11. As your heart rate increases, <u>one's</u> body receives more oxygen to help it accomplish strenuous tasks.

11. A) NO CHANGE
    B) their
    C) your
    D) our

_____ 12. Carina has moved her lambs into a larger enclosure where <u>there</u> going to have plenty of room as they get bigger.

12. A) NO CHANGE
    B) which
    C) they're
    D) their

_____ 13. Although Monopoly is extremely well-known, many board game enthusiasts claim <u>its'</u> too long and relies too much on randomness.

13. A) NO CHANGE
    B) its
    C) it's
    D) their

_____ 14. Molly and Hannah decided to start making money by teaching <u>their</u> dog to do tricks in front of an audience.

14. A) NO CHANGE
    B) they're
    C) there
    D) whose

_____ 15. If the planning committee had asked <u>Benjamin and myself</u> for help, they could have avoided the embarrassing incident with the ostrich and the chocolate fountain.

15. A) NO CHANGE
    B) myself and Benjamin
    C) Benjamin and I
    D) Benjamin and me

CONTINUE

# Math: Algebraic Manipulation

_____ **16.** If $D = ST$, which of the following expressions gives $S$ in terms of $D$ and $T$?

    A)  $S = DT$

    B)  $S = \dfrac{D}{T}$

    C)  $S = \dfrac{T}{D}$

    D)  $S = \dfrac{D}{T^2}$

_____ **17.** Given the formula $V = \pi r^2 h$, which of the following expressions gives the height ($h$) of the cylinder?

    A)  $h = \dfrac{V}{\pi r^2}$

    B)  $h = \dfrac{\pi r^2}{V}$

    C)  $h = \dfrac{\pi}{V r^2}$

    D)  $h = \dfrac{1}{\pi r^2 V}$

_____ **18.** Given the formula $a = \dfrac{v - u}{t}$, what is $v$ in terms of $a$, $t$, and $u$?

    A)  $v = \dfrac{u}{at}$

    B)  $v = \dfrac{at}{u}$

    C)  $v = u - at$

    D)  $v = u + at$

_____ **19.** Given the formula $T = 2\pi\sqrt{\dfrac{L}{g}}$, what is $L$ in terms of $T$ and $g$?

    A)  $L = \dfrac{4\pi r^2}{T^2 g}$

    B)  $L = \dfrac{Tg}{2\pi}$

    C)  $L = \dfrac{T^2 g}{4\pi^2}$

    D)  $L = \dfrac{T^2 g}{2\pi^2}$

_____ **20.** The formula $F = \dfrac{9}{5}C + 32$ gives the temperature in Fahrenheit in terms of Celsius. Which of the following expression gives the temperature in Celsius in terms of Fahrenheit?

    A)  $C = (F - 32)\dfrac{5}{9}$

    B)  $C = (F - 32)\dfrac{9}{5}$

    C)  $C = \dfrac{5}{9}F - 32$

    D)  $C = \dfrac{9}{5}F + 32$

**CONTINUE**

# Math: Systems of Equations

_____ **21.** What are the solutions for the equations
$-x + 2y = -10$ and $2 - 6y = 5x$ ?

A) $x = -4, y = 3$
B) $x = -3, y = 4$
C) $x = 3, y = -4$
D) $x = 4, y = -3$

_____ **22.** What values of $a$ and $b$ satisfy the system of equations below?

$$-3a - 9b = -15$$
$$7a - 3b = \phantom{-}59$$

A) $a = -8, b = 1$
B) $a = -1, b = 8$
C) $a = 8, b = -1$
D) $a = 8, b = 1$

_____ **23.** What values of $m$ and $n$ satisfy the system of equations below?

$$3m + 5n = \phantom{-}-6$$
$$-2m + 7n = \phantom{-}4$$

A) $m = -2 , n = -2$
B) $m = 0 , n = -2$
C) $m = -2 , n = 0$
D) $m = 2 , n = 0$

_____ **24.** What values of $p$ and $q$ satisfy the system of equations below?

$$\frac{p-q}{2} = p + 3$$
$$p + 5 = q + 3$$

A) $p = -4 , q = -3$
B) $p = -4, q = -2$
C) $p = -2, q = -4$
D) $p = 2, q = 4$

_____ **25.** What values of $c$ and $d$ satisfy the system of equations below?

$$5c - 5d = \phantom{-}5$$
$$4c - 3d = \phantom{-}13$$

A) $c = 10, d = 9$
B) $c = 9, d = 10$
C) $c = -9, d = 10$
D) $c = -10, d = -9$

**STOP**

# Homework 5

## Reading: Explicit Questions 1

*Gravitational waves* are changes in the curvature of space-time, moving at light-speed, that are initiated by accelerating bodies found within binary star systems.
*Line* These bodies can be neutron stars, white dwarf stars, or
*5* black holes. When, for example, binary neutron stars orbit close to each other, the extremely large acceleration of their masses form gravitational waves. An observer would notice rhythmic (wave-like) distortions in local space-time. Distances between
*10* objects would fluctuate with the frequency of the wave.

So do these waves actually affect Earth? The short answer is yes, but because of the astronomical distances involved, the effect is so minuscule that only the most sensitive devices can measure the effect. The first
*15* observation of a gravitational wave was made on September 14th, 2015. Two black holes, each about 30 times more massive than our sun, had spiraled and merged, creating an unimaginably powerful wave that finally reached us after traveling through a billion light
*20* years of space. By the time it got here, it was detected by a device whose 4-kilometer arm changed in length by the unimaginably small distance of ten-thousandths of the width of a proton.

**MAIN IDEA:** _____

_____

_____ 1. According to the passage, the gravitational wave that scientists were first able to observe was:

**ANTICIPATION:** _____

_____

A) created by an event that took place in 2015.
B) found within the orbit of neutron stars.
C) created through the interactions of two black holes.
D) measured to be approximately 4-kilometers long.

_____ 2. The passage states that the large acceleration of massive objects in space:

**ANTICIPATION:** _____

_____

A) can alter the way that space and time appear to behave.
B) can cause binary star systems to orbit each other more closely.
C) typically produce fluctuations in local space-time conditions that are observable from Earth.
D) are responses to curvatures in space-time.

CONTINUE ➡

# Reading: Explicit Questions 2

Because of their size, microbes are easy to underestimate, but microbiology is one of the most rewarding areas of study within the field of biology, as micro-
*Line* biologists work toward discovering new microbes and
5 learning about the stunning and varied ways they interact with other living organisms, ourselves included. To see their importance, consider the fact that the average adult has about 40 trillion bacteria in or on their bodies. That's about 10 trillion more than the number of
10 cells found inside each of us. Consider further that for *most of the history of life on Earth,* the tiny microbe was the only kind of life there was.

One key realization that has begun to seep into the consciousness of non-biologists is that microbes are not
15 simply invisible carriers of disease. Some certainly are lethal and terrifyingly infectious, but many of them benefit people and other animals to the point that we couldn't exist without them. Furthermore, life of any kind would be a shaky matter without the microbes that
20 take care of biogeochemical decomposition and that are a crucial part of producing the oxygen we breathe.

**MAIN IDEA:** _____

_____

_____ **3.** The passage states that each of the following is true about microbes EXCEPT that:

**ANTICIPATION:** _____

_____

A) adults have more microbes than cells in their body.
B) there are more different types of microbes than any other form of life.
C) microbes have been on the planet longer than any other form of life.
D) they have a wide range of ability to interact with other life forms.

_____ **4.** According to the passage, microbiologists are working to:

**ANTICIPATION:** _____

_____

A) create microbes that are beneficial to humans.
B) convince non-scientists that not all microbes are dangerous to humans.
C) discover the existence of new microbes.
D) determine the way microbes generate biogeochemical decomposition.

CONTINUE ➤

# Reading: Vocab-in-context Questions 1

Donald looked at Tim Capulsky, slumped in front of the television in his hotel room watching the local news. He eyed this man who was his friend, client, and
*Line*
5 very possibly the next senator of New Jersey, and was glad to see him inert for a change. It was an exhausting day, and tomorrow wouldn't be much better. Donald had the urge to turn off the TV and carry him to his bed and tuck him in. He chuckled softly at the image and Capulsky turned around but said nothing. Once the
10 program turned from politics to gossip, the candidate stretched and shut the TV off. He looked at his friend.

"Don't worry. I'm happy. May not look it right now, but I'm happy. I'm definitely pleased with all you've been doing. Sometimes I want to tell the folks,
15 'Hey, if you like me, you'll really like the guy whose doing most of the heavy lifting—the brains of the outfit' and then dragging you to the podium."

"Don't do that."

They both smiled almost the exact same smile. An
20 unwelcome rapping at the door broke the moment and Capulsky put a finger to his lips. He made a head-on-pillow gesture and backed his way into his bedroom, saluting his good night. Donald nodded his approval and readied his own excuse as he approached the door.

**MAIN IDEA:** _____

_____

_____ **5.** Which of the following is closest to the meaning of *inert* as it is used in line 5?

**ANTICIPATION:** _____

_____

A) motionless
B) asleep
C) inoperative
D) exhausted

_____ **6.** Which of the following is closest to the meaning of *readied* as it is used in line 24?

**ANTICIPATION:** _____

_____

A) began
B) remembered
C) prepared
D) embellished

CONTINUE ➤

# Reading: Vocab-in-context Questions 2

The state of the art of jazz playing and composition is healthy and productive. The current level of musicianship is impressive: an arresting number of young players today can handle traditional bebop, post-bebop, and more modern, rock-influenced idioms. While some neo-traditionalists such as Wynton Marsalis once called for increased respect for the past and attention to one's craft, such controversies have settled down of late. People feel less inclined to choose sides, and traditionalism sits comfortably with a more forward-thinking, globally-informed sound that nods to the free jazz of the 1960s.

Some believe this means that there is not now, and never again can be, a jazz avant-garde. There is only a safe, innocuous sound and approach that, whatever pleasures it affords and whatever superficial differences exist between performers and pieces, has become so encompassing that nothing will again seem startlingly, brashly, even annoyingly ahead of its time. I suspect that the time is now ripe for just such a phenomenon, but I am less sure that anyone will take advantage of the opportunity.

*Line 5*
*10*
*15*
*20*

**MAIN IDEA:** _____

_____

_____ **7.** As it is used in line 3, *arresting* most nearly means:

**ANTICIPATION:** _____

_____

A) decreasing
B) impressive
C) halting
D) implausible

_____ **8.** As it is used in line 15, *innocuous* most nearly means:

**ANTICIPATION:** _____

_____

A) bland
B) painless
C) similar
D) inventive

CONTINUE

# Math: Algebra

_____ **9.** If $3x + 5 = 17$, $x = ?$

A) 3
B) 4
C) 5
D) 6

_____ **10.** If $5x - 13 = 32$, $x = ?$

A) 9
B) 10
C) 11
D) 12

_____ **11.** If $4x - 21 = 56 - 3x$, $x = ?$

A) 3
B) 5
C) 9
D) 11

_____ **12.** If $\dfrac{3x + 8}{2} = 16$, $x = ?$

A) 5
B) 6
C) 7
D) 8

_____ **13.** If $3(2x - 9) = 15$, $x = ?$

A) 1
B) 4
C) 5
D) 7

_____ **14.** If $\sqrt{x - 9} = 2$, $x = ?$

A) −3
B) 3
C) 13
D) 23

_____ **15.** If $(x - 5)(x + 6) = x^2$, $x = ?$

A) 15
B) 20
C) 25
D) 30

_____ **16.** $4y + 5x + 14 = 2y + 7x + 20$, what is $y$ in terms of $x$?

A) $y = x - 3$
B) $y = x + 3$
C) $y = 2x + 4$
D) $y = 2x + 6$

$$2a + b = \quad 9$$
$$3b + c = \quad 25$$
$$2a + 3c = \quad 14$$

_____ **17.** Given the system of equations above, what is the value of $a + b + c$ ?

A) 8
B) 10
C) 12
D) 16

_____ **18.** If $x + y = 10$ and $x^2 - y^2 = 60$, what is the value of $x - y$ ?

A) 6
B) 8
C) 10
D) 12

**STOP**

# Homework 6

## Reading: Inferential Questions 1

The sight of the mimic octopus living up to its name is one of the most extraordinary in all of nature. Other animals have impressive abilities to change their appearance to resemble different animals or blend in with their surroundings, as do all species of octopus to some extent, but *Thaumoctopus mimicus* is, as far we know, unsurpassed in the range of its mimicry. It is believed to be able to imitate fifteen other local marine organisms.

*Line 5*

It is not just the general shape and coloring of an animal that this octopus imitates. When, for example, it mimics a flounder or jellyfish, it moves in a manner uncannily like these creatures. Perhaps not surprisingly, given its relative vulnerability, the mimic octopus is particularly adept at taking on the appearance of poisonous or venomous animals. It can, for example, mimic a poisonous sea snake by burying all but two of its legs in the ocean floor, and then extending these two out straight.

*10*

*15*

**MAIN IDEA:** _____

_____

_____ **1.** It can reasonably be inferred from the passage that the mimic octopus lacks the ability to:

**ANTICIPATION:** _____

_____

A) use venom to defend itself.
B) imitate animals that prey upon it.
C) mimic plant life.
D) bury itself completely in the ocean floor.

_____ **2.** It can be inferred from paragraph 1 that other species of octopus besides the mimic octopus can:

**ANTICIPATION:** _____

_____

A) change their appearance in less impressive ways than the mimic octopus.
B) imitate the shape and coloring of the mimic octopus.
C) move or behave like the organisms they are mimicking.
D) imitate up to fifteen other local marine organisms.

CONTINUE ➡

# Reading: Inferential Questions 2

Detective fiction occupies a curious position in the literary world. The commercial success of so many contemporary authors writing within the genre attests to
*Line* its wide appeal. Furthermore, critical respectability has
5 long been accorded to a number of detective novelists, starting with Poe, who wrote the prototype of the detective in Auguste Dupin, down to Hammett and Chandler with their stories of tough guys and tougher dames. However, admiration for these writers stems less
10 from the cleverness of their plots—ostensibly the genre's main appeal—than for their literary style. The more mundane detective novel, the whodunit, still gets little respect.

What then to make of George Simenon, another
15 successful author and original stylist, praised by the likes of Henry Miller, but, unlike Hammett and Chandler, never fully embraced by devotees of detective fiction? It may be that Simenon's talent was so thorough-going that his slim novels, regardless of the
20 presence of criminals, police detectives, and all the rest, seem self-contained and unrelated to works of any other kind. He was not a genre author or a self-consciously anti-genre author, a situation that must frustrate those who read detective works as a sort of hobby.

**MAIN IDEA:** _____

_____

_____ **3.** It can be inferred from the passage that Simenon's novels:

**ANTICIPATION:** _____

_____

A) were not truly detective novels because they only infrequently featured detectives.
B) were stylistically superior to those of other writers working within the detective novel genre.
C) were popular with people who did not typically read detective novels.
D) did not feature the tough guys and women of the works of Hammett and Chandler.

_____ **4.** The passage suggests that the author believes that Henry Miller was:

**ANTICIPATION:** _____

_____

A) wrote with a better literary style than Hammett and Chandler.
B) someone whose approval signified artistic merit.
C) a well-known fan of detective fiction.
D) a successful author who rarely read detective fiction.

CONTINUE ➡

# Reading: Strategy Questions 1

The popularity of so-called personality tests used to help evaluate potential new employees or to get a better sense of how current employees think and feel about
Line their job is a depressing phenomenon. The effectiveness
5 of the tests, whether given on paper or online, whether they take 10-minutes or all day, is wholly unsubstantiated. A newly published paper that looked at new hires at five major businesses that use these tests shows no correspondence between high scores in test
10 results and worker productivity. The authors of the paper point to numerous weaknesses in each of the different tests used and are not afraid to point out the obvious: self-deception and outright lying render the tests virtually useless.

15 Furthermore, the authors state, giving these tests to current employees is an almost sure-fire way to erode trust. Nearly 70% of test-takers, who were assured that their remarks would be kept confidential, said that taking the tests made them feel less valued as workers.
20 81% said that sitting for about 20 minutes with their supervisors would have been a more effective way to convey their true thoughts about their work. For those who view that statistic skeptically, 85% of their employers said the same thing.

**MAIN IDEA:** _____

_____

_____ 5. Which of the following statements best describes the structure of the passage?

**ANTICIPATION:** _____

_____

A) It contradicts a widely-held idea and then explores the reasons why that idea gained popularity.
B) It states an opinion about a popular procedure and then supports that opinion with relevant data.
C) It presents a summary of a research paper and then questions its results using personal stories.
D) It shows the flaws of a certain practice and then suggests possible improvements to it.

_____ 6. The last sentence of the passage serves to:

**ANTICIPATION:** _____

_____

A) summarize the major point made in the second paragraph.
B) emphasize the ineffectiveness of a type of business research.
C) give an example of how data can be misinterpreted.
D) provide a piece of data that anticipates an objection.

CONTINUE ➡

# Reading: Main Idea Questions 3

In musical theater, a collection of top-notch songs dwelling within a second-rate story will not last long. Conversely, a compelling drama or truly funny script that comes with some hit-and-miss songs can be a winner. Story, it seems, trumps tune for winning over both audiences and critics. This holds true even for today's "jukebox musicals," shows built around well-loved pop songs. One would think they'd be immune to concerns about story, since the songs are the whole point of the show. Yet, the most successful of these productions are still those in which story delivers the engaging characters, dramatic situations, and few good laughs.

*Line*
*5*

*10*

All of which underscores the importance of the "book writer," yet the public still lacks a definite understanding of what these folks do and how they contribute to a show's success. Book writers write the story itself: the plot, setting, dialogue, and anything outside of the music and lyrics. Book writers create the people who inhabit a show. Glorious melodies and clever song lyrics will not much move an audience if put into the mouths of dull or underdeveloped characters. The book writer gives the songwriters the substance to which they can add their art.

*15*

*20*

**MAIN IDEA:** _____

_____

_____ 7. The main idea of the first paragraph is:

**ANTICIPATION:** _____

_____

A) top-notch songs are crucial to the success of a musical.
B) jukebox musicals are the only shows that do not heavily rely on story.
C) no musical without a strong story and top-notch songs is likely to be successful.
D) the quality of the story is more important to a musical's success than that of its songs.

_____ 8. The main idea of the second paragraph is:

**ANTICIPATION:** _____

_____

A) few people are aware of how important book writers are to jukebox musicals.
B) book writers are unappreciated but crucial to the success of musicals.
C) the music and lyrics to a musical is usually less substantial than the story itself.
D) a musical is unlikely to be successful if the characters in the show are not fully three-dimensional.

CONTINUE

**Name:** _____  **Date:** _____

# Math: Function Notation

**Questions 9 to 14 refer to the following function:**

| Let $h(x) = x^2 + 3x$ |
|---|

_____ **9.** $h(2) = ?$

- A) 5
- B) 7
- C) 10
- D) 12

_____ **10.** $h(3) = ?$

- A) 6
- B) 9
- C) 12
- D) 18

_____ **11.** $h(-2) = ?$

- A) −10
- B) −2
- C) −1
- D) 10

_____ **12.** $h(7) = ?$

- A) 28
- B) 49
- C) 52
- D) 70

_____ **13.** $h(0) = ?$

- A) −3
- B) 0
- C) 3
- D) 9

_____ **14.** If $h(k) = 0$, which of the following could be the value of $k$?

- A) −3
- B) −1
- C) 3
- D) 9

**Questions 15 to 18 refer to the following function:**

| Let $f(x) = (x - 3)^2$ |
|---|
| Let $g(x) = 2x - 1$ |

_____ **15.** $f(5) = ?$

- A) 2
- B) 4
- C) 8
- D) 16

_____ **16.** $f(12) = ?$

- A) 9
- B) 18
- C) 27
- D) 81

_____ **17.** $g(8) = ?$

- A) 15
- B) 17
- C) 19
- D) 23

_____ **18.** If $g(4) = a$, what is $f(a)$?

- A) 1
- B) 7
- C) 15
- D) 16

**CONTINUE**

# Math: FOIL

_____ **19.** $(x + 3)(x + 2) = ?$

    A) $x^2 + x + 5$
    B) $x^2 + 5x + 5$
    C) $x^2 + 5x + 6$
    D) $x^2 + 6x + 5$

_____ **20.** $(x + 4)(x - 1) = ?$

    A) $x^2 + 3x - 4$
    B) $x^2 + 3x + 3$
    C) $x^2 + 5x - 4$
    D) $x^2 - 3x - 4$

_____ **21.** $(x - 5)(x - 6) = ?$

    A) $x^2 - x - 11$
    B) $x^2 - x - 30$
    C) $x^2 + 11x + 30$
    D) $x^2 - 11x + 30$

_____ **22.** $(x - 2)(x + 1) = ?$

    A) $x^2 + x - 2$
    B) $x^2 - x + 2$
    C) $x^2 - x - 2$
    D) $x^2 - 2x - 2$

_____ **23.** $(2x - 1)(x + 3) = ?$

    A) $2x^2 + 2x - 3$
    B) $2x^2 + 5x - 3$
    C) $2x^2 + 6x - 3$
    D) $2x^2 + 7x + 3$

_____ **24.** $(3x + 5)(4x - 2) = ?$

    A) $7x^2 + 3x - 10$
    B) $7x^2 + 14x - 10$
    C) $12x^2 + 7x + 10$
    D) $12x^2 + 14x - 10$

_____ **25.** $(2x - 3)(7x - 4) = ?$

    A) $9x^2 - 7x + 12$
    B) $9x^2 - 13x - 1$
    C) $14x^2 - 29x - 12$
    D) $14x^2 - 29x + 12$

_____ **26.** $(10x + 3)(5x + 12) = ?$

    A) $15x^2 + 135x + 36$
    B) $15x^2 + 150x + 15$
    C) $50x^2 + 135x + 36$
    D) $50x^2 + 150x + 120$

_____ **27.** $(5x - 1)(-3x + 8) = ?$

    A) $-15x^2 + 43x - 8$
    B) $-15x^2 - 37x - 8$
    C) $15x^2 - 43x + 8$
    D) $15x^2 + 37x - 8$

_____ **28.** $(-2x + 9)(-4x + 10) = ?$

    A) $-8x^2 - 56x + 90$
    B) $-8x^2 - 36x - 20$
    C) $8x^2 - 56x + 90$
    D) $8x^2 - 36x + 90$

**STOP**

# Homework 7

## Writing: Fragments 1

_____ 1. Waffles, though primarily served at breakfast in America, <u>but eaten</u> throughout the day in Belgium.

    1. A) NO CHANGE
       B) eaten
       C) are eaten
       D) eating

_____ 2. The launch of the new <u>website, already delayed</u> three weeks when the developers were forced to postpone it indefinitely.

    2. A) NO CHANGE
       B) website; it was already delayed
       C) website was already delayed
       D) website, which was already delayed

_____ 3. Nepal's national <u>flag, which is the world's only non-rectangular national flag and also</u> the only flag that is taller than it is wide.

    3. A) NO CHANGE
       B) flag, which is the world's only non-rectangular national flag and which is
       C) flag, the world's only non-rectangular national flag, as well as
       D) flag is the world's only non-rectangular national flag and also

_____ 4. The northern cardinal, <u>one of the most common birds in North America, and also</u> the official bird of seven different U.S. states.

    4. A) NO CHANGE
       B) one of the most common birds in North America, is
       C) which is one of the most common birds in North America and
       D) which is one of the most common birds in North America and is

_____ 5. Harry Beck's landmark 1931 map of the London Underground rail <u>system depicting</u> train lines only in straight lines with orthogonal angles, with no reference to actual geography or topology.

    5. A) NO CHANGE
       B) system depicted
       C) system that depicted
       D) system; it depicted

CONTINUE ➤

# Writing: Fragments 2

_____ **6.** Dwayne Johnson, also known as The <u>Rock, who has</u> made a skillful transition from professional wrestler to Hollywood actor.

**6.** A) NO CHANGE
B) Rock, having
C) Rock, and who has
D) Rock, has

_____ **7.** If the school's administrators are serious about increasing <u>enrollment. They</u> should take a hard look at where they're spending their money.

**7.** A) NO CHANGE
B) enrollment, they
C) enrollment; they
D) enrollment,

_____ **8.** In Myanmar, the military <u>having excluded Aung San Suu Kyi,</u> the leader of the country's democratic movement, from holding the office of president.

**8.** A) NO CHANGE
B) has excluded Aung San Suu Kyi,
C) having excluded Aung San Suu Kyi, who is
D) excluding Aung San Suu Kyi,

_____ **9.** Even though the forecast didn't call for <u>rain, Mary still packed</u> an umbrella for her vacation, knowing that the local climate was highly unpredictable.

**9.** A) NO CHANGE
B) rain. Mary still packed
C) rain, Mary still packing
D) rain, but Mary still packed

_____ **10.** Descending deeper and deeper into the murky depths, Jordan Summers, the leader of the scuba diving tour, <u>while keeping</u> a close eye on the less experienced divers in her group.

**10.** A) NO CHANGE
B) keeping
C) kept
D) who kept

CONTINUE →

**Name:** _____  **Date:** _____

# Writing: Run-Ons 1

_____ 11. Andrew Johnson was impeached by the House of Representatives in <u>1868, then he was acquitted</u> in the Senate by one vote, allowing him to continue his term as President of the United States.

11. A) NO CHANGE
    B) 1868, he was acquitted
    C) 1868; acquitted
    D) 1868; however, he was acquitted

_____ 12. Despite their image as a quintessentially American fruit, apples were first cultivated in Kazakhstan in central Asia, <u>China is the largest apple producer today.</u>

12. A) NO CHANGE
    B) China produces apples in the largest number today
    C) and China is the largest apple producer today
    D) today it is China that produces the most apples

_____ 13. It had been twenty years since Shelly had visited her <u>hometown, she feared</u> what it had become in the time she was gone.

13. A) NO CHANGE
    B) hometown; she being afraid of
    C) hometown, and she feared
    D) hometown, therefore she feared

_____ 14. <u>Jeff initially did not feel prepared for the test,</u> he had no trouble with any of the questions once it started.

14. A) NO CHANGE
    B) Jeff's initial feeling was that he was not prepared for the test
    C) Initially, Jeff felt that he was not prepared for the test
    D) Although Jeff initially did not feel prepared for the test

_____ 15. Most people consider George Washington to be America's first President, but some argue it was technically John <u>Hanson, he was President of the Continental Congress</u> under the Articles of Confederation from 1781 to 1782.

15. A) NO CHANGE
    B) Hanson, who was President of the Continental Congress
    C) Hanson, the President of the Continental Congress was
    D) Hanson; President of the Continental Congress

# Writing: Run-Ons 2

_____ 16. We have to bring a lot of equipment to the practice field <u>tomorrow it</u> would be easier to take my car.

16. A) NO CHANGE
    B) tomorrow, it
    C) tomorrow, therefore, it
    D) tomorrow, so it

_____ 17. Nina's new restaurant buys ingredients from local producers whenever <u>possible, however, some</u> foods just can't be grown outside of a tropical climate.

17. A) NO CHANGE
    B) possible, some
    C) possible; however, some
    D) possible, nevertheless some

_____ 18. <u>Tensions in Europe were rising on the eve of World War I, no one</u> could have predicted that the sovereignty dispute between Austria and Serbia would lead to a conflict that would embroil the whole continent.

18. A) NO CHANGE
    B) Although tensions in Europe were rising on the eve of World War I, no one
    C) Tensions in Europe had risen on the eve of World War I, no one
    D) Tensions in Europe had risen on the eve of World War I, however no one

_____ 19. Because Warren loved to swim, he decided to take his vacation in the <u>Caribbean, the water is</u> much clearer and warmer than those near his home in Virginia.

19. A) NO CHANGE
    B) Caribbean, where the water is
    C) Caribbean the water there can be
    D) Caribbean, its waters are

_____ 20. Terry Gross has been a staple for National Public Radio for over forty <u>years, her</u> show "Fresh Air" continues to be one of the network's most popular programs.

20. A) NO CHANGE
    B) years, and her
    C) years, it is her
    D) years her

CONTINUE

# Math: Factoring

_____ **21.** The expression $(3x - 2)(5x + 8)$ is equivalent to:

   A) $15x^2 - 14x - 16$
   B) $15x^2 + 14x - 16$
   C) $15x^2 - 14x + 16$
   D) $15x^2 - 16$

_____ **22.** Which of the following expressions is equivalent to $10x^2 + 25x + 15$ ?

   A) $(x + 10)(x + 15)$
   B) $(x - 1)(10x + 15)$
   C) $(x + 1)(10x + 15)$
   D) $(x - 1)(15x - 10)$

_____ **23.** Which of the following expressions is equivalent to: $16x^2 + 8x + 1 = 0$ ?

   A) $(4x + 1)^2$
   B) $(4x + 1)(4x - 1)$
   C) $(4x - 1)^2$
   D) $(1 - 4x)^2$

_____ **24.** Which of the following expressions is a factored form of $6xy^5 + 3x^5y$ ?

   A) $6x^4y^4$
   B) $6xy(y^4 + x^4)$
   C) $3xy(2y^4 + x^4)$
   D) $3x^4y^4(2y + x)$

_____ **25.** Which of the following choices shows all of the positive factors of the number 16?

   A) 1, 2, 4, 8, 16
   B) 1, 2, 4, 16
   C) 1, 2, 4, 12, 32
   D) 1, 8, 16, 32

_____ **26.** Which of the following expressions is equivalent to $(x + 3)(x^2 + 3x - 5)$ ?

   A) $x^3 + 6x^2 + 4x - 15$
   B) $x^3 + 3x^2 + 12x - 15$
   C) $x^3 + 3x^2 + 9x - 15$
   D) $x^3 + 6x^2 + 2x - 15$

_____ **27.** Which of the following expressions is equivalent to $6x^2 + 5x - 6$ ?

   A) $(3x - 2)(3x + 3)$
   B) $(3 - 2x)(2 - 3x)$
   C) $(2x - 3)(3x + 2)$
   D) $(2x + 3)(3x - 2)$

_____ **28.** Which of the following expressions is equivalent to $x^2 - 25$ ?

   A) $(x + 5)(x + 5)$
   B) $(x + 5)(x - 5)$
   C) $(x + 5)^2$
   D) $(x - 5)^2$

_____ **29.** The expression given below is equivalent to which of the following expressions $8x^2 - 22x - 21$ ?

   A) $(2x + 7)(4x - 3)$
   B) $(2x - 7)(4x + 3)$
   C) $(7x + 2)(3x - 4)$
   D) $(7x - 2)(3x + 4)$

_____ **30.** Which of the following choices shows all of the positive factors of the number 18?

   A) 1, 3, 4, 6, 9, 18
   B) 1, 3, 6, 9, 12
   C) 1, 2, 6, 9, 36
   D) 1, 2, 3, 6, 9, 18

**STOP**

# Homework 8

## Writing: Commas 1

_____ 1. As the lead scientist on the university's new nanobot research <u>team, Dr. Neilson</u> found she spent more time managing the other researchers than doing experiments herself.

1. A) NO CHANGE
   B) team Dr. Neilson,
   C) team, Dr. Neilson,
   D) team; Dr. Neilson

_____ 2. King Leopold II of <u>Belgium, founded a brutally exploitative</u> "Free State" in the Congo by convincing other Europeans that he was engaged in humanitarian work.

2. A) NO CHANGE
   B) Belgium founded, a brutally exploitative
   C) Belgium founded a brutally exploitative
   D) Belgium, founded a brutally exploitative,

_____ 3. John Carpenter's gruesome horror <u>movie *The Thing* made in 1982,</u> is often considered the apex of achievement in practical special effects.

3. A) NO CHANGE
   B) movie *The Thing* made in 1982
   C) movie, *The Thing* made in 1982
   D) movie *The Thing*, made in 1982,

_____ 4. Anybody who knew Stella could tell <u>you that she loved,</u> her dog, her music, and her beat-up pickup truck.

4. A) NO CHANGE
   B) you that, she loved
   C) you, that she loved,
   D) you that she loved

_____ 5. The ascension of Maria Theresa to the throne of <u>Austria, led directly to the War of Austrian Succession,</u> which lasted almost eight years and embroiled most of Europe's great powers.

5. A) NO CHANGE
   B) Austria led directly to the War of Austrian Succession,
   C) Austria led directly, to the War of Austrian Succession
   D) Austria, led directly to the War of Austrian Succession

CONTINUE →

# Writing: Commas 2

_____ **6.** Andy always preferred to go to the <u>beach, on the north side</u> of the harbor because it was usually less crowded.

**6.** A) NO CHANGE
B) beach on the north side,
C) beach, on the north side,
D) beach on the north side

_____ **7.** Capable of reaching speeds over two hundred miles per <u>hour, the peregrine falcon is the fastest animal on Earth,</u> an honor many mistakenly bestow on the cheetah.

**7.** A) NO CHANGE
B) hour the peregrine falcon is the fastest animal on Earth,
C) hour the peregrine falcon is the fastest animal on Earth
D) hour, the peregrine falcon, is the fastest animal on Earth

_____ **8.** Many of my friends believe that the old mental <u>hospital an abandoned building, across the street, from our school</u> is haunted.

**8.** A) NO CHANGE
B) hospital, an abandoned building across the street from our school,
C) hospital, an abandoned building across the street, from our school
D) hospital an abandoned building, across the street, from our school,

_____ **9.** Melissa's grandfather was a renowned crime-scene <u>photographer, in Chicago, and,</u> she has decorated her apartment with dozens of his most interesting works.

**9.** A) NO CHANGE
B) photographer, in Chicago and
C) photographer in Chicago, and
D) photographer in, Chicago and

_____ **10.** Before he created <u>Mario possibly the most famous video game character of all time,</u> Shigeru Miyamoto was employed by Nintendo to create artwork that would adorn arcade machines.

**10.** A) NO CHANGE
B) Mario, possibly the most famous video game character of all time,
C) Mario, possibly, the most famous video game character of all time
D) Mario, possibly the most famous video game character, of all time

CONTINUE

# Writing: Apostrophes 1

_____ 11. The unfortunate nexus of air <u>current's in the office meant Yvonne's</u> desk was always freezing when the air conditioning was active.

11. A) NO CHANGE
    B) current's in the office meant Yvonnes
    C) currents' in the office meant Yvonnes
    D) currents in the office meant Yvonne's

_____ 12. By design, it's difficult to determine where this <u>sentences' apostrophes</u> should be placed.

12. A) NO CHANGE
    B) sentence's apostrophes
    C) sentences apostrophes'
    D) sentence's apostrophe's

_____ 13. The <u>scientists' noses'</u> all wrinkled in unison when confronted with the ghastly results of their attempt to design a new deodorant.

13. A) NO CHANGE
    B) scientists nose's
    C) scientists' noses
    D) scientist's noses

_____ 14. In the raffle, Taylor won a <u>series of cooking lessons from the restaurant's</u> gregarious head chef.

14. A) NO CHANGE
    B) series of cooking lessons' from the restaurant's
    C) series' of cooking lessons from the restaurants
    D) series of cooking lesson's from the restaurants

_____ 15. The <u>neighborhoods criminal elements</u> don't stand a chance against its newest hero!

15. A) NO CHANGE
    B) neighborhoods' criminal elements
    C) neighborhood's criminal elements
    D) neighborhoods criminal elements'

CONTINUE →

# Writing: Other Punctuation 1

_____ **16.** My friend Naomi—a pediatric surgeon at the local children's <u>hospital,</u> is one of the hardest-working people I know.

**16.** A) NO CHANGE
B) hospital
C) hospital;
D) hospital—

_____ **17.** Simon Bolivar dreamed of a unified and democratic South <u>America, however,</u> in the years immediately after his death, foreign intervention and political infighting quickly dissolved that dream.

**17.** A) NO CHANGE
B) America however;
C) America; however,
D) America, however—

_____ **18.** Before the invention of printing <u>press, creating</u> a new book involved hundreds of hours of meticulous copying by hand, often done by monks.

**18.** A) NO CHANGE
B) press. Creating
C) press: creating
D) press; creating

_____ **19.** Despite the dramatically increasing cost of rent, having increased by more than fifty percent over the last five <u>years—</u>people continue to move to New York City at record rates.

**19.** A) NO CHANGE
B) years,
C) years;
D) years:

_____ **20.** Building new subway lines can be expensive <u>business, if we want to increase capacity and remain in the black,</u> we should focus on refining the service on our existing infrastructure.

**20.** A) NO CHANGE
B) business; if we want to increase capacity and remain in the black;
C) business; if we want to increase capacity and remain in the black,
D) business if we want to increase capacity and remain in the black,

# Math: Graphing Functions

_____ **21.** What is the slope of the line that passes through the points $(1, 2)$ and $(3, 8)$ ?

- A) $-3$
- B) $-1/3$
- C) $1/3$
- D) $3$

_____ **22.** What is the slope of the line that passes through the points $(-6, 4)$ and $(1, -3)$ ?

- A) $-7/6$
- B) $-6/7$
- C) $-1$
- D) $1$

_____ **23.** What is the $y$-intercept of the line that passes through the points $(1, -1)$ and $(5, 7)$ ?

- A) $-3$
- B) $-2$
- C) $-1$
- D) $1$

_____ **24.** What is the $x$-intercept of the line that passes through the points $(1, -1)$ and $(5, 7)$ ?

- A) $1/2$
- B) $3/2$
- C) $5/2$
- D) $7/2$

_____ **25.** The equation of line $\ell$ is $y = 3x + 7$. If line $k$ is perpendicular to line $\ell$, what is the slope of line $k$?

- A) $-3$
- B) $-1/3$
- C) $1/3$
- D) $3/7$

_____ **26.** The equation of line $\ell$ is $y = 3x - 1$. If line $m$ is the reflection of line $\ell$ across the $x$-axis, what is the slope of line $m$?

- A) $-3$
- B) $-1/3$
- C) $-1$
- D) $1/3$

_____ **27.** The equation of line $\ell$ is $y = -2x + 3$. If line $k$ is parallel to line $\ell$ and passes through the point $(3,5)$, what is the $y$-intercept of line $k$?

- A) $8$
- B) $9$
- C) $10$
- D) $11$

**CONTINUE**

_____ **28.** Which of the following could be the graph of

$$y = -\frac{1}{2}x + 2 ?$$

A)                              B)

C)                              D)

_____ **29.** Which of the following could be the graph of
$y = 2x - 3$ ?

A)                              B)

C)                              D)

_____ **30.** Let the function $f$ be defined by

$f(x) = ax^2 + bx + c$ where $a$, $b$, and $c$ are
constants. If $a < 0$ and $c > 0$, then which of the
following could be the graph of $f$?

A)                              B)

C)                              D)

**STOP**

# Homework 9

## Reading: Double Passage 1

**Passage 1**

Not many Americans today can name one living serious composer (though with a little prodding, they might offer up John Williams, noted creator of the music
Line accompanying the Star Wars movies and other
5 blockbusters). People still attend concerts and operas, but the make-up of the audience doesn't bode well for the future of the art. The average age of a typical concertgoer has been on the rise for decades, and attempts to supplant this graying demographic with younger folks
10 has had limited success, especially from an artistic perspective. Putting together a family-friendly program by including popular songs, movie music, etc., does nothing to further the art form that the orchestras and concert halls were created to serve.

**Passage 2**

15 The current condition of concert music in the U.S. might be described as anemic, with a number of factors contributing to its decline. Ticket prices can be prohibitively high, especially the young. Fewer people of any age play instruments—musically literate non-
20 professionals have long made up a sizable portion of regular concertgoers. But the music itself has to take some of the blame as well. The at-times excruciatingly difficult music that became fashionable in the mid-20$^{th}$ century delivered a body blow to concert attendance that
25 is still being felt. But there is reason for optimism. We've seen a resurgence of ear-pleasing but still adventurous music from a growing clutch of youngish composers. Whether the younger folks who enthusiastically attend concerts of this music can spread the word
30 to those in their demographic who never step foot in a concert hall has yet to be determined.

---

_____ **1.** Passages 1 and 2 both make the point that:

A) classical music does not have a sufficiently large audience among young people.
B) fewer classical music fans today listen to music created by young composers.
C) the artistic quality of classical music concerts had been on the decline for years.
D) classical music concerts designed for younger audiences have been unpopular.

_____ **2.** Unlike the author of Passage 1, the author of Passage 2:

A) makes the case that attendance at classical music concerts is likely to increase.
B) criticizes composers from the recent past for writing music that was not adventurous.
C) points out that people today are less musically knowledgeable.
D) addresses causes for a decline in interest in classical music.

---

**MAIN IDEAS:**

A: _____

B: _____

CONTINUE →

# Reading: Double Passage 2

**Passage 1**

Amid the general concern over climate change, there has been less focus on rainforest deforestation. Deforestation, especially in the Amazon, is of course, a significant driver of global warming: the ldeoss of trees, which consume carbon dioxide, leads to greater amounts of carbon in the air, leading in turn to more heat being trapped in Earth's lower atmosphere.

However, other serious dangers arise from the indiscriminate slash-and-burn approach that continues to be used in the Amazon by loggers and others. The indigenous people have been treated roughly, at times brutally, as their homelands have been destroyed or made uninhabitable. The number of plant and animal species continues to decline at a rate estimated at 50,000 species annually. Deforestation also typically leads to soil erosion, and once fertile areas turn into wasteland.

**Passage 2**

A number of steps have been taken to curb the serious environmental dangers associated with deforestation. One of the most common-sense approaches involves a stricter monitoring of forest loss. Arial photographs can be studied by individuals who do not possess advanced training. Satellite images of so-called hot spots, areas most susceptible to rapid loss, can be analyzed. These methods can be used to track regrowth as well as forest loss.

Another important advance is the development of new farming methods that minimize the amount of deforested land needed by small local farmers by showing them how to increase crop yield. A particularly inventive method for accomplishing this is the creation of food forests that replicate natural forests. These agroforestal systems have proved successful at reducing dependence on fossil fuels and chemicals and improving the quality of the local soil and water. More importantly, this is both a pragmatic and an ethical way to keep in mind the rights of the people who have lived in the forest all their lives.

*Line* 5, 10, 15, 20, 25, 30, 35

**3.** Both passages mention the people who have always lived in the rainforest, but only Passage 2:

A) involves them in ways to remedy the problem of deforestation.
B) explains how they have helped formulate ways to alleviate the problem of deforestation.
C) states that they have been treated brutally at times in the past.
D) acknowledges that there has been a lessening of habitat loss due to deforestation in recent years.

**4.** It can be inferred from the passage that the author of Passage 2 would most likely:

A) feel that the author of Passage 1 has overstated the threat posed by deforestation.
B) strongly agree with the concerns expressed by the author of Passage 1.
C) argue that the solutions proposed by the author of Passage 1 are impractical.
D) point out that climate change is only one threat posed by deforestation.

**MAIN IDEAS:**

A: _____

B: _____

CONTINUE

# Math: Averages

_____ 5. Three dogs weigh an average of 60 pounds. If two of those dogs weigh an average of 50 pounds, how much does the third dog weigh?

    A) 50
    B) 55
    C) 60
    D) 80

_____ 6. 10 people own an average of 10 dogs. If 8 of these people have an average of 2 dogs, what is the average number of dogs for the remaining 2 people?

    A) 6
    B) 12
    C) 24
    D) 42

**Questions 7 to 10 refer to the following table:**

| BOB'S HOUSE OF PANTS | |
| --- | --- |
| City | Number of stores |
| Baltimore | 7 |
| Buffalo | 3 |
| Cleveland | 8 |
| New York | 9 |
| Pittsburgh | 3 |

Bob's House of Pants has stores in five U.S. cities, as shown in the table above.

_____ 7. What is the average number of stores in these cities?

    A) 3
    B) 4
    C) 5
    D) 6

_____ 9. Bob's House of Pants plans to expand, opening 10 stores in Indianapolis. After this expansion, what will the median number of stores be in all cities in the U.S.?

    A) 7
    B) 7.5
    C) 8
    D) 8.5

_____ 8. What is the median number of stores in these cities?

    A) 6
    B) 6.5
    C) 7
    D) 7.5

_____ 10. In addition to the expansion described in the previous question, Bob's House of Pants will expand to a seventh city, opening 16 stores in Memphis. What will the new average number of stores be in all cities in the U.S.?

    A) 8
    B) 9
    C) 10
    D) 11

CONTINUE

**Questions 11 to 14 refer to the following table:**

| KANSAS CITY COWS<br>Last week's games | | | | |
|---|---|---|---|---|
| Date | Opponent | Runs scored | Runs allowed | Result |
| Monday | Wichita | 7 | 1 | Win |
| Tuesday | Omaha | 4 | 3 | Win |
| Wednesday | Omaha | 4 | 5 | Loss |
| Thursday | Omaha | 2 | 1 | Win |
| Friday | Tulsa | 10 | 7 | Win |
| Saturday | Tulsa | 6 | 7 | Loss |

The table above shows the results of six games played by the Kansas City Cows baseball team last week. "Runs scored" shows the number of runs the Cows scored in each game, while "Runs allowed" shows the number of runs the opponent scored.

_____ 11. What is the average number of runs scored by the Cows in games last week?

A) 5
B) 5.5
C) 6
D) 6.5

_____ 13. What was the average number of runs scored by the Cows in games against Tulsa last week?

A) 4
B) 6
C) 8
D) 10

_____ 12. What was the median number of runs allowed by the Cows in games last week?

A) 3
B) 3.5
C) 4
D) 4.5

_____ 14. What was the average number of runs scored by the Cows in games they won last week?

A) 5
B) 5.25
C) 5.5
D) 5.75

CONTINUE

# Math: Probability

_____ **15.** A certain jar contains 100 total coins. If 40 of the coins are pennies, what is the probability that a coin chosen at random is a penny?

A) 1/100
B) 1/40
C) 1/25
D) 2/5

_____ **16.** Gregor has some kittens, 8 of which are grey. If he picks one of his kittens at random, the probability that he chose a grey kitten is 2/3. How many total kittens does Gregor have?

A) 4
B) 6
C) 12
D) 16

_____ **17.** There are 24 cars in a parking lot. If a car is selected at random, the probability that it is blue is 5/8. How many cars in the parking lot are <u>not</u> blue?

A) 3
B) 9
C) 12
D) 15

_____ **18.** A store sells shirts in three sizes: Small, Medium, and Large. The store has 11 Small shirts and 7 Medium shirts. If the probability of randomly choosing a Large shirt is 1/3, how many total shirts does the store have?

A) 6
B) 9
C) 18
D) 27

{ 1, 3, 5, 6, 7, 8, 10, 11, 15, 16 }

_____ **19.** If $k$ is a number chosen at random from the set above, what is the probability that $k$ is divisible by 5?

A) 1/5
B) 2/5
C) 3/9
D) 3/10

**STOP**

# Homewor k 10

## Writing: Redundancy 1

_____ 1. Every year, our glee club's annual charity benefit raises money to fund music education in poor countries around the world.

    1.  A) NO CHANGE
         B) Once a year, our
         C) Our
         D) As a yearly charity event, our

_____ 2. Last year my family took a trip to the Netherlands, and I was amazed by the clean public parks there that were so neat.

    2.  A) NO CHANGE
         B) parks there in the Netherlands.
         C) tidily there in the Netherlands.
         D) parks.

_____ 3. Owen and Logan are pooling their money to buy an advanced digital camera, so they can film the movie script that Owen wrote.

    3.  A) NO CHANGE
         B) he wrote.
         C) Owen wrote for a movie.
         D) was written by him for them to film.

_____ 4. Isabel knew that she shouldn't open the strange, rumbling box that was making noise in the corner of her grandparent's attic.

    4.  A) NO CHANGE
         B) odd, rumbling box that was strange
         C) strange, rumbling box
         D) odd and strange box

_____ 5. Pyramids can be found around the world. They were often built by slaves and usually served as religious buildings across the globe.

    5.  A) NO CHANGE
         B) buildings globally.
         C) buildings.
         D) structures anywhere in the world.

CONTINUE ➡

# Writing: Redundancy 2

_____ 6. Stringed instruments played by hand have existed for thousands of years, but the first instruments with recognizable similarities to modern guitars were created in Spain in the 13th century. <u>They have traits in common with modern guitars.</u>

6. A) NO CHANGE
   B) These Spanish instruments share a number of traits with modern guitars.
   C) Modern guitars have a number of similarities to them.
   D) DELETE the underlined portion.

_____ 7. Because his car broke down, all week my friend has found himself in the <u>unfortunate and luckless position</u> of needing to ask his older brother for a ride to work.

7. A) NO CHANGE
   B) unfortunate position
   C) unlucky position for the whole week
   D) lucklessly unfortunate position

_____ 8. Our local tennis <u>club, which serves the nearby area,</u> is planning a tournament for Labor Day weekend.

8. A) NO CHANGE
   B) club
   C) club of tennis players
   D) club, which plays tennis,

_____ 9. Victoria eased past the old marble statue and <u>carefully avoided touching its marble form with great care</u> to prevent it from collapsing.

9. A) NO CHANGE
   B) with great care avoided touching or contacting it
   C) carefully avoided touching it
   D) using great care avoided any contact so as not to touch the statue

_____ 10. Sierra was very proud of her encyclopedic knowledge of mid-nineties television shows and was <u>happy</u> to demonstrate it at parties.

10. A) NO CHANGE
    B) happy and amicable
    C) happy to show and
    D) DELETE the underlined portion.

CONTINUE

# Writing: Transitions 1

____ **11.** Robert the Bald defeated Prince Ethelrood at the Battle of the Three Rivers. He was, <u>however,</u> able to the prince's throne by right of conquest.

**11.** A) NO CHANGE
B) nevertheless,
C) therefore,
D) previously,

____ **12.** When it comes to running the restaurant, my boss micromanages us way too much. <u>Nevertheless,</u> he makes us account for where every lemon slice goes, and he refuses to let anyone else fold the napkins.

**12.** A) NO CHANGE
B) On the other hand,
C) For example,
D) Surprisingly,

____ **13.** The Brontë sisters—Charlotte, Emily, and Anne—may very well make up the most talented family of writers in human history. <u>All three</u> enjoyed success as poets and novelists.

**13.** A) NO CHANGE
B) However, all three
C) All three, in contrast,
D) Therefore, all three

____ **14.** <u>Because</u> the Berlin Wall was brought down more than 25 years ago, differences between the two halves of the city remain.

**14.** A) NO CHANGE
B) Although
C) Before
D) If

____ **15.** The research team believes there may be a link between low rainfall and the migration routes of geese. <u>For example,</u> they will tag several specimens to track whether the geese appear in areas that have recently experienced drought.

**15.** A) NO CHANGE
B) Nevertheless,
C) Coincidentally,
D) For this reason,

CONTINUE

# Writing: Transitions 2

_____ **16.** To celebrate the 4th of July, the city council has planned a giant parade and a million-dollar fireworks spectacle. The whole plan may be in jeopardy, <u>additionally,</u> if this torrential rain refuses to stop.

**16.** A) NO CHANGE
B) therefore,
C) for instance,
D) however,

_____ **17.** Because there is disagreement about what level of soccer counts as "professional", it is difficult to determine the leading scorer of all time. <u>Conversely,</u> some sources name Pelé as having the most goals while others believe it to be Josef Bican.

**17.** A) NO CHANGE
B) On the other hand,
C) Consequently,
D) At that time,

_____ **18.** *Turritopsis dohrnii* is a species of jellyfish that is able to revert from its adult state back to an immature polyp at any time. <u>In light of this ability,</u> the species is called the "immortal jellyfish."

**18.** A) NO CHANGE
B) Despite this talent,
C) That is because
D) Surprisingly, this means

_____ **19.** Theories about the true authorship of Shakespeare's plays are plentiful. In the academic community, <u>therefore,</u> proposed alternative authors are rarely taken seriously, as there is no concrete evidence to suggest any of them wrote the plays.

**19.** A) NO CHANGE
B) as one example,
C) similarly,
D) however,

_____ **20.** At the annual harvest festival, the villagers would bring all their crops to the square to be judged, <u>while</u> those chosen as the finest would be brought to the temple at the top of the mountain.

**20.** A) NO CHANGE
B) although
C) during which
D) after which

CONTINUE →

# Math: Technique Review

**DIRECTIONS: You must use an SAT math technique** on each of the following questions. You must indicate which technique you used—either **Plug In** or **Backsolve**—and show your work.

_____ 21. Alvin, Barney, and Cedric made a total of 18 sandwiches to bring to a picnic. Alvin made 2 more sandwiches than Barney made, and Cedric made 3 times as many as Alvin. How many sandwiches did Barney make?

A)  2
B)  4
C)  6
D)  10

_____ 22. **Technique used:**

A)  Plug In
B)  Backsolve

_____ 23. If Arthur was $y$ years old exactly 3 years ago, how old will he be in exactly $x$ years?

A)  $x + y$
B)  $x + y - 3$
C)  $x - y - 3$
D)  $x + y + 3$

_____ 24. **Technique used:**

A)  Plug In
B)  Backsolve

_____ 25. The high road to Scotland is 180 miles longer than the low road. When Jocelyn goes to Scotland by the high road and returns along the low road, the round trip is 1,060 miles. How many miles is the high road?

A)  350
B)  440
C)  530
D)  620

_____ 26. **Technique used:**

A)  Plug In
B)  Backsolve

_____ 27. If $a$, $b$, and $c$ are consecutive even integers such that $a < b < c$, which of the following is equal to $a^2 + b^2 + c^2$?

A)  $3b^2 + 2$
B)  $3b^2 + 6$
C)  $3b^2 + 8$
D)  $3b^2 + 6b + 5$

_____ 28. **Technique used:**

A)  Plug In
B)  Backsolve

_____ 29. It takes Donna 4 minutes to grade an essay, and it takes Clay 6 minutes to grade an essay. If they both start working at the same time, how many minutes will it take them to grade 20 total essays?

A)  40
B)  48
C)  72
D)  100

_____ 30. **Technique used:**

A)  Plug In
B)  Backsolve

**STOP**

# Course C

**3 hr 24 hr**

## Reading: Passage 1

Most people use the word "hobo" as little more than a derogatory term for the homeless, deriding them as lazy bums who spend their days idly wandering the country. However, the word properly refers to an itinerant worker. Far from lazy, hobos travel hundreds of miles looking for any work they can find. When jobs were especially scarce during the Great Depression several hundred thousand hobos traveled from town to town, hitching rides in railway freight cars and carrying only the bare essentials on their backs. As their numbers increased, hobo culture became more organized, developing ways to communicate with each other to keep safe. These included homemade travel books and a system of written symbols to inform other hobos whether nearby houses were friendly or hostile. Today, hobos even have their own union and an annual convention in Britt, Iowa, home of the National Hobo Museum.

*Line 5*

*10*

*15*

**MAIN IDEA:** _____

_____

_____ **1.** In context, the author includes lines 1-4 ("Most... country") in order to

**ANTICIPATION:** _____

_____

A) present a common opinion the author will refute
B) demonstrate the proper connotation of a word
C) disparage the indolence of the hobo lifestyle
D) detail the history of itinerant workers in the U.S.

_____ **2.** The "books" (line 13) and the "system" (line 14) are given as examples of

**ANTICIPATION:** _____

_____

A) objects that can be seen in the National Hobo Museum
B) the dangers that hobos can encounter on the road
C) methods hobos use for interacting with their peers
D) tools needed to perform a typical job that a hobo finds

CONTINUE ➡

Name: _____ Date: _____

Americans are spoiled by the mutual intelligibility of the regional variations of their language. The differences between dialects within the country are trivial, such as whether a carbonated beverage is called "soda" or "pop" or whether "caramel" should be pronounced with two syllables or three. When compared with other languages, American English shows astonishing little variation. In Germany, for example, there are over a dozen distinct Germanic languages spoken, from Alemannic to Westphalian, some of which have deep grammatical differences beyond simple vocabulary or phonology. The difference can be starker with German spoken in other countries: the "German" spoken in Switzerland is practically incomprehensible to one who speaks only Standard German. When Americans travel in America, other people may sound funny, but they understand each other. If a German strays too far from home, the people around him might as well be speaking Latin.

*Line*
5

10

15

**MAIN IDEA:** _____

_____

_____ 3. The author says Americans are "spoiled" (line 1) because they

**ANTICIPATION:** _____

_____

A) struggle to learn many different varieties of American English
B) use different words for common things than people from other parts of the country
C) have little difficulty understanding each other compared with people in other countries
D) speak a language that has no variation across the country

_____ 4. In line 19, "Latin" serves as an example of a language that

**ANTICIPATION:** _____

_____

A) has significant dialectical variation
B) is a dialect spoken within Germany
C) only varies in simple vocabulary and phonology
D) is so foreign that it is incomprehensible

CONTINUE ➤

# Reading: Passage 3

George Balanchine is rightly remembered as one of the greatest choreographers of our time, but his muses, the women who inspired him, are just as deserving of
*Line*
acclaim. He seemingly was never without a muse, from
5  Vera Zorina in Broadway musicals and Hollywood films, to prima ballerina Maria Tallchief in *The Nutcracker* and *Swan Lake*, to Suzanne Farrell in *Meditation* and *Don Quixote*. These women did not simply perform his work: the work itself would not exist
10  without them. Unlike a painter or a writer, a choreographer like Balanchine is only one of many contributors to an artwork, and his muses can actively shape the result. The dancers are directed by his designs, but his designs are also transformed by their dancing.
15  Each of Balanchine's works merged his artistic vision with a different dancer's soul and spirit.

**MAIN IDEA:** _____

_____

_____ **5.** The author of the passage argues that Balanchine's "muses" (line 2)

**ANTICIPATION:** _____

_____

A) believed they did not get recognition for their contributions
B) deserve more credit than Balanchine for the value of his work
C) significantly contributed to Balanchine's work
D) were not sufficiently appreciated by Balanchine

_____ **6.** In lines 10-13 ("Unlike … the result") the author suggests

**ANTICIPATION:** _____

_____

A) painters and writers do not generally have muses
B) Balanchine was unhappy about his lack of control over his work
C) female painters and writers have fewer opportunities than female dancers
D) some artists have greater effect on their own work than Balanchine had

CONTINUE ➡

**Name:** _____ **Date:** _____

# Math: Plug In

**DIRECTIONS: You must use Plug In** on each of the following questions. Write your answer in the space before the question number.

_____ 7. Alan has $x$ chocolate bars and gets 10 more bars. He gives away half of his chocolate, and then gets another 10 bars. In terms of $x$, how many chocolate bars does Alan now have?

A) $x + 15$
B) $x + 20$
C) $\dfrac{x}{2}$
D) $\dfrac{x}{2} + 15$

_____ 8. If $a$ is 5 less than twice $b$, which of the following gives $b$ in terms of $a$?

A) $2a - 5$
B) $5 + 2a$
C) $\dfrac{5 - a}{2}$
D) $\dfrac{a + 5}{2}$

_____ 9. Stewart's car can hold a maximum of $g$ gallons in its gas tank, and gas costs $c$ dollars per gallon. If the car currently has 2 gallons of gas in the tank, what is the cost, in dollars, to fill up the rest of the tank?

A) $cg - 2$
B) $cg - 2c$
C) $cg - 2g$
D) $g - 2c$

_____ 10. In a series of three numbers, the second number is 3 less than the first, and the third is three times the second. If the first number is $x$, how much greater than the second number is the third number?

A) $2x - 6$
B) $2x - 9$
C) $2x - 12$
D) $3x - 3$

_____ 11. Olivia earns a commission of 15 percent of the price of every boat she sells. Which of the following gives the amount of her commission, in dollars, if she sells $x$ boats that each cost $y$ dollars?

A) $15xy$
B) $1500xy$
C) $\dfrac{3xy}{20}$
D) $\dfrac{3y}{20x}$

# STOP

# Homework 2

## Writing: Verbs 1

_____ 1. My best friend, who enjoys making music and plays several instruments, <u>plan</u> to visit Maine this winter and write songs in a cabin.

1.  A) NO CHANGE
    B) have planned
    C) are planning
    D) plans

_____ 2. When they worked together at the library, Naomi and Nicholas <u>hunt</u> through the aisles for books with ridiculous names.

2.  A) NO CHANGE
    B) will hunt
    C) would hunt
    D) are hunting

_____ 3. It looks like our hike might be cut short because a swarm of angry bees <u>have blocked</u> the trail ahead.

3.  A) NO CHANGE
    B) is blocking
    C) would block
    D) are blocking

_____ 4. In 1965, Soviet cosmonaut Alexey Leonov <u>will perform</u> the first extra-vehicular space walk in human history.

4.  A) NO CHANGE
    B) performs
    C) performed
    D) has performed

_____ 5. The dulcet tones of the piano that had been drifting across the restaurant to the table where Danny waited for his date <u>were</u> suddenly drowned out by the sound of a blender running in the kitchen.

5.  A) NO CHANGE
    B) has been
    C) was
    D) is

**CONTINUE**

# Writing: Verbs 2

_____ 6. In Professor Tomlin's lab, a team of undergraduate students have found a way to "listen" to space by monitoring radio waves as they travel through the cosmic void.

6. A) NO CHANGE
   B) are finding
   C) find
   D) has found

_____ 7. Past the stone monument that marks the end of the beach, lies two tide pools that glitter beautifully in the moonlight.

7. A) NO CHANGE
   B) lie
   C) has lied
   D) is

_____ 8. Next spring, the Emergency Response Team created by the previous mayor has been replaced by a smaller Emergency Dispatch Service that will direct existing resources to respond to crises.

8. A) NO CHANGE
   B) was
   C) is
   D) will be

_____ 9. The requests that Joanna's employees made— on a number of topics but most notably for more vacation time—were reasonable, so she happily changed her policies.

9. A) NO CHANGE
   B) would be
   C) was
   D) is

_____ 10. Because it had been containing private details about his own life and family, Eugene O'Neill's masterpiece *A Long Day's Journey Into Night* was not published until after his death.

10. A) NO CHANGE
    B) contained
    C) will contain
    D) has contained

CONTINUE

# Writing: Pronouns 1

_____ 11. All the apartments in the new buildings have a new washing machine for the convenience of <u>it's</u> occupants.

11. A) NO CHANGE
    B) their
    C) its
    D) there

_____ 12. I thought this coat looked great on me at the store, but when I got home I found that <u>it's</u> not exactly the color I expected.

12. A) NO CHANGE
    B) its
    C) its'
    D) they're

_____ 13. Ian loved the look of his new phone, but disliked <u>its'</u> lack of features.

13. A) NO CHANGE
    B) their
    C) its
    D) it's

_____ 14. Every meeting of the Iowa Misanthrope Club ends with a vote for a new chairperson, <u>whom</u> would be forced to host the next meeting.

14. A) NO CHANGE
    B) who
    C) which
    D) whose

_____ 15. If one wishes to build a successful business, <u>they</u> should carefully consider how to stand out from competing ventures.

15. A) NO CHANGE
    B) we
    C) you
    D) one

CONTINUE ➤

# Writing: Pronouns 2

_____ **16.** The school's new policy allows students to easily obtain a copy of <u>their</u> attendance or academic records at any point during the year.

**16.**
A) NO CHANGE
B) his or her
C) they're
D) your

_____ **17.** Paul and Olivia liked how <u>they're</u> new back yard opened up directly to a meadow with a tiny stream.

**17.**
A) NO CHANGE
B) its
C) there
D) their

_____ **18.** The hippopotamus, despite having an innocuous appearance, is actually extremely dangerous and can kill with <u>their</u> powerful bite.

**18.**
A) NO CHANGE
B) they're
C) its
D) it's

_____ **19.** Scientists at NASA are planning a mission to bring an asteroid into lunar orbit so <u>they</u> can be studied more easily by astronauts.

**19.**
A) NO CHANGE
B) it
C) which
D) them

_____ **20.** After the conclusion of the piano recital, the teacher asked <u>my friend and I</u> to play a duet together as the audience left the auditorium.

**20.**
A) NO CHANGE
B) my friend and me
C) I and my friend
D) my friend and myself

CONTINUE

**Name:** _____ **Date:** _____

# Math: Backsolve

**DIRECTIONS: You must use Backsolve** on each of the following questions. Write your answer in the space before the question number.

_____ **21.** Tree X is 23 inches tall and tree Y is 73 inches tall. Tree X grows 5 inches a year and tree Y grows 3 inches a year. In how many years will tree X be the same height as tree Y?

    A) 10
    B) 15
    C) 25
    D) 30

$$a + b = 17$$
$$b + c = 35$$
$$a + c = 28$$

_____ **24.** In the system of equations above, what is the value of $a$?

    A) 5
    B) 10
    C) 12
    D) 24

_____ **22.** At a movie theater, small drinks cost \$3 each and large drinks cost \$5 each. The theater sells 100 total drinks for a total of \$380. How many small drinks were sold?

    A) 45
    B) 50
    C) 55
    D) 60

_____ **25.** Molly has 36 more red shirts than blue shirts. Half the number of red shirts equals twice the number of blue shirts. How many blue shirts does she have?

    A) 9
    B) 12
    C) 24
    D) 36

$$B(d) = 2d^2 + 10$$

_____ **23.** The function $B$, defined above, models the number of new bees born in a beehive after $d$ days. According to this model, how many days would it take for the colony to gain 108 new bees?

    A) 4
    B) 5
    C) 6
    D) 7

CONTINUE ➡

# Math: Fundamentals Review

_____ **26.** If $\dfrac{a}{2} \times \dfrac{1}{8} = \dfrac{\frac{3}{4}}{6}$, then $a = ?$

A) 2
B) 3
C) 4
D) 6

_____ **27.** What is the remainder when 52 is divided by 3?

A) 0
B) 1
C) 2
D) 3

_____ **28.** A recipe calls for 3 cups of flour for every 5 cups of sugar. If Bill uses 15 cups of flour, how many cups of sugar should he use?

A) 10
B) 15
C) 20
D) 25

_____ **29.** A certain park contains only maple and elm trees in a ratio of 2 to 3, respectively. If there are a total of 40 trees, how many elm trees are there in the park?

A) 16
B) 18
C) 20
D) 24

_____ **30.** What percent of 40 is 8?

A) 5
B) 10
C) 20
D) 30

_____ **31.** 9 is 15 percent of what number?

A) 60
B) 70
C) 75
D) 80

_____ **32.** Joe made 160 dollars last week and 180 dollars this week. What was the percent increase in his pay?

A) 10
B) 12.5
C) 15
D) 17.5

_____ **33.** $x^3 \left( x^2 \right)^5 = ?$

A) $x^5$
B) $x^7$
C) $x^{10}$
D) $x^{13}$

_____ **34.** If $d^3 \times d^4 = d^p$ and $\dfrac{d^{12}}{d^6} = d^q$, what is $p + q$?

A) 1
B) 6
C) 7
D) 13

_____ **35.** If $|x - 6| = 23$, which of the following gives all possible values of $x$?

A) $-29$
B) $-17$
C) $-17$ and 29
D) 17 and $-29$

**STOP**

# Homework 3

## Reading: Explicit Questions 1

*Gravitational waves* are changes in the curvature of space-time, moving at light-speed, that are initiated by accelerating bodies found within binary star systems.

*Line*
*5* These bodies can be neutron stars, white dwarf stars, or black holes. When, for example, binary neutron stars orbit close to each other, the extremely large acceleration of their masses form gravitational waves. An observer would notice rhythmic (wave-like) distortions in local space-time. Distances between
*10* objects would fluctuate with the frequency of the wave.

So do these waves actually affect Earth? The short answer is yes, but because of the astronomical distances involved, the effect is so minuscule that only the most sensitive devices can measure the effect. The first
*15* observation of a gravitational wave was made on September 14th, 2015. Two black holes, each about 30 times more massive than our sun, had spiraled and merged, creating an unimaginably powerful wave that finally reached us after traveling through a billion light
*20* years of space. By the time it got here, it was detected by a device whose 4-kilometer arm changed in length by the unimaginably small distance of ten-thousandths of the width of a proton.

**MAIN IDEA:** _____

_____

_____ 1. According to the passage, the gravitational wave that scientists were first able to observe was:

**ANTICIPATION:** _____

_____

A) created by an event that took place in 2015.
B) found within the orbit of neutron stars.
C) created through the interactions of two black holes.
D) measured to be approximately 4-kilometers long.

_____ 2. The passage states that the large acceleration of massive objects in space:

**ANTICIPATION:** _____

_____

A) can alter the way that space and time appear to behave.
B) can cause binary star systems to orbit each other more closely.
C) typically produce fluctuations in local space-time conditions that are observable from Earth.
D) are responses to curvatures in space-time.

CONTINUE ➡

# Reading: Vocab-in-context Questions 1

Donald looked at Tim Capulsky, slumped in front of the television in his hotel room watching the local news. He eyed this man who was his friend, client, and

Line very possibly the next senator of New Jersey, and was
5 glad to see him inert for a change. It was an exhausting day, and tomorrow wouldn't be much better. Donald had the urge to turn off the TV and carry him to his bed and tuck him in. He chuckled softly at the image and Capulsky turned around but said nothing. Once the
10 program turned from politics to gossip, the candidate stretched and shut the TV off. He looked at his friend.

"Don't worry. I'm happy. May not look it right now, but I'm happy. I'm definitely pleased with all you've been doing. Sometimes I want to tell the folks,
15 'Hey, if you like me, you'll really like the guy whose doing most of the heavy lifting—the brains of the outfit' and then dragging you to the podium."

"Don't do that."

They both smiled almost the exact same smile. An
20 unwelcome rapping at the door broke the moment and Capulsky put a finger to his lips. He made a head-on-pillow gesture and backed his way into his bedroom, saluting his good night. Donald nodded his approval and readied his own excuse as he approached the door.

MAIN IDEA: _____

_____

_____ 3. Which of the following is closest to the meaning of *inert* as it is used in line 5?

ANTICIPATION: _____

_____

A) motionless
B) asleep
C) inoperative
D) exhausted

_____ 4. Which of the following is closest to the meaning of *readied* as it is used in line 24?

ANTICIPATION: _____

_____

A) began
B) remembered
C) prepared
D) embellished

CONTINUE ►

# Reading: Main Idea Questions 1

Vegetarianism in on the rise in virtually all demographic groups in the United States and in much of the rest of the world. Even more impressive is the rate of increase in the percentage of the U.S. population that has substantially cut back on their animal product intake. These changes are not fads: analysts of every segment of the food industry agree that the American diet has irrevocably altered.

The reasons for this are many and overlapping. Nutrition and animal well-being, not surprisingly, are the most often cited, but increasingly, recent converts to vegetarianism mention cost, weight loss, food safety, and religious proscriptions as motivating factors. Interestingly, the reason most often given by *non*-vegetarians for why they choose to remain meat-eaters—taste—also plays a role in the decision of others to forego animal products. In the last ten years, food manufacturers have become more skilled at producing easy-to-prepare vegetarian items that simply taste delicious.

*Line* numbers: 5, 10, 15, 20

**MAIN IDEA:** _____

_____

_____ **5.** The primary function of the first paragraph is to:

**ANTICIPATION:** _____

_____

A) briefly describe the how the food industry tracks vegetarianism.
B) explain that the United States has started a worldwide rise in vegetarianism.
C) show that the author approves in the rise in vegetarianism.
D) identify the trend that people in the United States eat less meat and will continue to do so.

_____ **6.** The main purpose of the second paragraph is to:

**ANTICIPATION:** _____

_____

A) give arguments in favor of the changes discussed in the first paragraph.
B) present an overview of a range of recent changes that have taken place in the American diet.
C) discuss changes in the manufacturing process of vegetarian meals.
D) provide possible explanations for the increase in vegetarianism.

CONTINUE →

# Reading: Inferential Questions 1

The sight of the mimic octopus living up to its name is one of the most extraordinary in all of nature. Other animals have impressive abilities to change their appearance to resemble different animals or blend in with their surroundings, as do all species of octopus to some extent, but *Thaumoctopus mimicus* is, as far we know, unsurpassed in the range of its mimicry. It is believed to be able to imitate fifteen other local marine organisms.

*Line 5*

It is not just the general shape and coloring of an animal that this octopus imitates. When, for example, it mimics a flounder or jellyfish, it moves in a manner uncannily like these creatures. Perhaps not surprisingly, given its relative vulnerability, the mimic octopus is particularly adept at taking on the appearance of poisonous or venomous animals. It can, for example, mimic a poisonous sea snake by burying all but two of its legs in the ocean floor, and then extending these two out straight.

*10*

*15*

**MAIN IDEA:** _____

_____

_____ 7. It can reasonably be inferred from the passage that the mimic octopus lacks the ability to:

**ANTICIPATION:** _____

_____

A) use venom to defend itself.
B) imitate animals that prey upon it.
C) mimic plant life.
D) bury itself completely in the ocean floor.

_____ 8. It can be inferred from paragraph 1 that other species of octopus besides the mimic octopus can:

**ANTICIPATION:** _____

_____

A) change their appearance in less impressive ways than the mimic octopus.
B) imitate the shape and coloring of the mimic octopus.
C) move or behave like the organisms they are mimicking.
D) imitate up to fifteen other local marine organisms.

CONTINUE

# Math: Algebra

_____ **9.** If $3x + 5 = 17$, $x = ?$

    A)  3
    B)  4
    C)  5
    D)  6

_____ **10.** If $5x - 13 = 32$, $x = ?$

    A)  9
    B)  10
    C)  11
    D)  12

_____ **11.** If $4x - 21 = 56 - 3x$, $x = ?$

    A)  3
    B)  5
    C)  9
    D)  11

_____ **12.** If $\dfrac{3x+8}{2} = 16$, $x = ?$

    A)  5
    B)  6
    C)  7
    D)  8

_____ **13.** If $3(2x - 9) = 15$, $x = ?$

    A)  1
    B)  4
    C)  5
    D)  7

_____ **14.** If $\sqrt{x - 9} = 2$, $x = ?$

    A)  −3
    B)  3
    C)  13
    D)  23

_____ **15.** If $(x - 5)(x + 6) = x^2$, $x = ?$

    A)  15
    B)  20
    C)  25
    D)  30

_____ **16.** $4y + 5x + 14 = 2y + 7x + 20$, what is $y$ in terms of $x$?

    A)  $y = x - 3$
    B)  $y = x + 3$
    C)  $y = 2x + 4$
    D)  $y = 2x + 6$

$$2a + b = 9$$
$$3b + c = 25$$
$$2a + 3c = 14$$

_____ **17.** Given the system of equations above, what is the value of $a + b + c$?

    A)  8
    B)  10
    C)  12
    D)  16

_____ **18.** If $x + y = 10$ and $x^2 - y^2 = 60$, what is the value of $x - y$?

    A)  6
    B)  8
    C)  10
    D)  12

**STOP**

# Homework 4

## Writing: Fragments 1

_____ 1. Waffles, though primarily served at breakfast in America, <u>but eaten</u> throughout the day in Belgium.

    1.  A) NO CHANGE
           B) eaten
           C) are eaten
           D) eating

_____ 2. The launch of the new <u>website, already delayed</u> three weeks when the developers were forced to postpone it indefinitely.

    2.  A) NO CHANGE
           B) website; it was already delayed
           C) website was already delayed
           D) website, which was already delayed

_____ 3. Nepal's national <u>flag, which is the world's only non-rectangular national flag and also</u> the only flag that is taller than it is wide.

    3.  A) NO CHANGE
           B) flag, which is the world's only non-rectangular national flag and which is
           C) flag, the world's only non-rectangular national flag, as well as
           D) flag is the world's only non-rectangular national flag and also

_____ 4. The northern cardinal, <u>one of the most common birds in North America, and also</u> the official bird of seven different U.S. states.

    4.  A) NO CHANGE
           B) one of the most common birds in North America, is
           C) which is one of the most common birds in North America and
           D) which is one of the most common birds in North America and is

_____ 5. Harry Beck's landmark 1931 map of the London Underground rail <u>system depicting</u> train lines only in straight lines with orthogonal angles, with no reference to actual geography or topology.

    5.  A) NO CHANGE
           B) system depicted
           C) system that depicted
           D) system; it depicted

**CONTINUE** →

**Name:** _____ **Date:** _____

# Writing: Run-Ons 1

_____ **6.** Andrew Johnson was impeached by the House of Representatives in <u>1868, then he was acquitted</u> in the Senate by one vote, allowing him to continue his term as President of the United States.

**6.** A) NO CHANGE
B) 1868, he was acquitted
C) 1868; acquitted
D) 1868; however, he was acquitted

_____ **7.** Despite their image as a quintessentially American fruit, apples were first cultivated in Kazakhstan in central Asia, <u>China is the largest apple producer today.</u>

**7.** A) NO CHANGE
B) China produces apples in the largest number today
C) and China is the largest apple producer today
D) today it is China that produces the most apples

_____ **8.** It had been twenty years since Shelly had visited her <u>hometown, she feared</u> what it had become in the time she was gone.

**8.** A) NO CHANGE
B) hometown; she being afraid of
C) hometown, and she feared
D) hometown, therefore she feared

_____ **9.** <u>Jeff initially did not feel prepared for the test,</u> he had no trouble with any of the questions once it started.

**9.** A) NO CHANGE
B) Jeff's initial feeling was that he was not prepared for the test
C) Initially, Jeff felt that he was not prepared for the test
D) Although Jeff initially did not feel prepared for the test

_____ **10.** Most people consider George Washington to be America's first President, but some argue it was technically John <u>Hanson, he was President of the Continental Congress</u> under the Articles of Confederation from 1781 to 1782.

**10.** A) NO CHANGE
B) Hanson, who was President of the Continental Congress
C) Hanson, the President of the Continental Congress was
D) Hanson; President of the Continental Congress

**CONTINUE** →

# Writing: Commas 1

_____ **11.** As the lead scientist on the university's new nanobot research <u>team, Dr. Neilson</u> found she spent more time managing the other researchers than doing experiments herself.

**11.** A) NO CHANGE
B) team Dr. Neilson,
C) team, Dr. Neilson,
D) team; Dr. Neilson

_____ **12.** King Leopold II of <u>Belgium, founded a brutally exploitative</u> "Free State" in the Congo by convincing other Europeans that he was engaged in humanitarian work.

**12.** A) NO CHANGE
B) Belgium founded, a brutally exploitative
C) Belgium founded a brutally exploitative
D) Belgium, founded a brutally exploitative,

_____ **13.** John Carpenter's gruesome horror <u>movie *The Thing* made in 1982,</u> is often considered the apex of achievement in practical special effects.

**13.** A) NO CHANGE
B) movie *The Thing* made in 1982
C) movie, *The Thing* made in 1982
D) movie *The Thing*, made in 1982,

_____ **14.** Anybody who knew Stella could tell <u>you that she loved,</u> her dog, her music, and her beat-up pickup truck.

**14.** A) NO CHANGE
B) you that, she loved
C) you, that she loved,
D) you that she loved

_____ **15.** The ascension of Maria Theresa to the throne of <u>Austria, led directly to the War of Austrian Succession,</u> which lasted almost eight years and embroiled most of Europe's great powers.

**15.** A) NO CHANGE
B) Austria led directly to the War of Austrian Succession,
C) Austria led directly, to the War of Austrian Succession
D) Austria, led directly to the War of Austrian Succession

CONTINUE →

# Writing: Apostrophes 1

_____ **16.** The unfortunate nexus of air <u>current's in the office meant Yvonne's</u> desk was always freezing when the air conditioning was active.

**16.** A) NO CHANGE
B) current's in the office meant Yvonnes
C) currents' in the office meant Yvonnes
D) currents in the office meant Yvonne's

_____ **17.** By design, it's difficult to determine where this <u>sentences' apostrophes</u> should be placed.

**17.** A) NO CHANGE
B) sentence's apostrophes
C) sentences apostrophes'
D) sentence's apostrophe's

_____ **18.** The <u>scientists' noses'</u> all wrinkled in unison when confronted with the ghastly results of their attempt to design a new deodorant.

**18.** A) NO CHANGE
B) scientists nose's
C) scientists' noses
D) scientist's noses

_____ **19.** In the raffle, Taylor won a <u>series of cooking lessons from the restaurant's</u> gregarious head chef.

**19.** A) NO CHANGE
B) series of cooking lessons' from the restaurant's
C) series' of cooking lessons from the restaurants
D) series of cooking lesson's from the restaurants

_____ **20.** The <u>neighborhoods criminal elements</u> don't stand a chance against its newest hero!

**20.** A) NO CHANGE
B) neighborhoods' criminal elements
C) neighborhood's criminal elements
D) neighborhoods criminal elements'

**CONTINUE**

# Writing: Other Punctuation 1

_____ 21. My friend Naomi—a pediatric surgeon at the local children's <u>hospital,</u> is one of the hardest-working people I know.

21. A) NO CHANGE
    B) hospital
    C) hospital;
    D) hospital—

_____ 22. Simon Bolivar dreamed of a unified and democratic South <u>America, however,</u> in the years immediately after his death, foreign intervention and political infighting quickly dissolved that dream.

22. A) NO CHANGE
    B) America however;
    C) America; however,
    D) America, however—

_____ 23. Before the invention of printing <u>press, creating</u> a new book involved hundreds of hours of meticulous copying by hand, often done by monks.

23. A) NO CHANGE
    B) press. Creating
    C) press: creating
    D) press; creating

_____ 24. Despite the dramatically increasing cost of rent, having increased by more than fifty percent over the last five <u>years—</u>people continue to move to New York City at record rates.

24. A) NO CHANGE
    B) years,
    C) years;
    D) years:

_____ 25. Building new subway lines can be expensive <u>business, if we want to increase capacity and remain in the black,</u> we should focus on refining the service on our existing infrastructure.

25. A) NO CHANGE
    B) business; if we want to increase capacity and remain in the black;
    C) business; if we want to increase capacity and remain in the black,
    D) business if we want to increase capacity and remain in the black,

CONTINUE

# Math: Function Notation

**Questions 26 to 31 refer to the following function:**

| Let $h(x) = x^2 + 3x$ |
| --- |

_____ **26.** $h(2) = ?$

    A)    5
    B)    7
    C)    10
    D)    12

_____ **27.** $h(3) = ?$

    A)    6
    B)    9
    C)    12
    D)    18

_____ **28.** $h(-2) = ?$

    A)    −10
    B)    −2
    C)    −1
    D)    10

_____ **29.** $h(7) = ?$

    A)    28
    B)    49
    C)    52
    D)    70

_____ **30.** $h(0) = ?$

    A)    −3
    B)    0
    C)    3
    D)    9

_____ **31.** If $h(k) = 0$, which of the following could be the value of $k$?

    A)    −3
    B)    −1
    C)    3
    D)    9

**Questions 32 to 35 refer to the following function:**

| Let $f(x) = (x - 3)^2$<br>Let $g(x) = 2x - 1$ |
| --- |

_____ **32.** $f(5) = ?$

    A)    2
    B)    4
    C)    8
    D)    16

_____ **33.** $f(12) = ?$

    A)    9
    B)    18
    C)    27
    D)    81

_____ **34.** $g(8) = ?$

    A)    15
    B)    17
    C)    19
    D)    23

_____ **35.** If $g(4) = a$, what is $f(a)$ ?

    A)    1
    B)    7
    C)    15
    D)    16

CONTINUE ➡

# Math: Factoring

_____ **36.** The expression $(3x - 2)(5x + 8)$ is equivalent to:

A) $15x^2 - 14x - 16$
B) $15x^2 + 14x - 16$
C) $15x^2 - 14x + 16$
D) $15x^2 - 16$

_____ **37.** Which of the following expressions is equivalent to $10x^2 + 25x + 15$ ?

A) $(x + 10)(x + 15)$
B) $(x - 1)(10x + 15)$
C) $(x + 1)(10x + 15)$
D) $(x - 1)(15x - 10)$

_____ **38.** Which of the following expressions is equivalent to: $16x^2 + 8x + 1 = 0$ ?

A) $(4x + 1)^2$
B) $(4x + 1)(4x - 1)$
C) $(4x - 1)^2$
D) $(1 - 4x)^2$

_____ **39.** Which of the following expressions is a factored form of $6xy^5 + 3x^5y$ ?

A) $6x^4y^4$
B) $6xy(y^4 + x^4)$
C) $3xy(2y^4 + x^4)$
D) $3x^4y^4(2y + x)$

_____ **40.** Which of the following choices shows all of the positive factors of the number 16?

A) $1, 2, 4, 8, 16$
B) $1, 2, 4, 16$
C) $1, 2, 4, 12, 32$
D) $1, 8, 16, 32$

_____ **41.** Which of the following expressions is equivalent to $(x + 3)(x^2 + 3x - 5)$ ?

A) $x^3 + 6x^2 + 4x - 15$
B) $x^3 + 3x^2 + 12x - 15$
C) $x^3 + 3x^2 + 9x - 15$
D) $x^3 + 6x^2 + 2x - 15$

_____ **42.** Which of the following expressions is equivalent to $6x^2 + 5x - 6$ ?

A) $(3x - 2)(3x + 3)$
B) $(3 - 2x)(2 - 3x)$
C) $(2x - 3)(3x + 2)$
D) $(2x + 3)(3x - 2)$

_____ **43.** Which of the following expressions is equivalent to $x^2 - 25$ ?

A) $(x + 5)(x + 5)$
B) $(x + 5)(x - 5)$
C) $(x + 5)^2$
D) $(x - 5)^2$

_____ **44.** The expression given below is equivalent to which of the following expressions
$8x^2 - 22x - 21$ ?

A) $(2x + 7)(4x - 3)$
B) $(2x - 7)(4x + 3)$
C) $(7x + 2)(3x - 4)$
D) $(7x - 2)(3x + 4)$

_____ **45.** Which of the following choices shows all of the positive factors of the number 18?

A) $1, 3, 4, 6, 9, 18$
B) $1, 3, 6, 9, 12$
C) $1, 2, 6, 9, 36$
D) $1, 2, 3, 6, 9, 18$

**STOP**

Name: _____  Date: _____

# Homework 5

## Reading: Double Passage 1

### Passage 1

Not many Americans today can name one living
serious composer (though with a little prodding, they
might offer up John Williams, noted creator of the music
*Line* accompanying the Star Wars movies and other
5 blockbusters). People still attend concerts and operas,
but the make-up of the audience doesn't bode well for
the future of the art. The average age of a typical concertgoer has been on the rise for decades, and attempts
to supplant this graying demographic with younger folks
10 has had limited success, especially from an artistic
perspective. Putting together a family-friendly program
by including popular songs, movie music, etc., does
nothing to further the art form that the orchestras and
concert halls were created to serve.

### Passage 2

'15    The current condition of concert music in the U.S.
might be described as anemic, with a number of factors
contributing to its decline. Ticket prices can be
prohibitively high, especially the young. Fewer people
of any age play instruments—musically literate non-
20 professionals have long made up a sizable portion of
regular concertgoers. But the music itself has to take
some of the blame as well. The at-times excruciatingly
difficult music that became fashionable in the mid-20$^{th}$
century delivered a body blow to concert attendance that
25 is still being felt. But there is reason for optimism.
We've seen a resurgence of ear-pleasing but still
adventurous music from a growing clutch of youngish
composers. Whether the younger folks who enthusiastically attend concerts of this music can spread the word
30 to those in their demographic who never step foot in a
concert hall has yet to be determined.

_____ 1.  Passages 1 and 2 both make the point that:

A)  classical music does not have a sufficiently
large audience among young people.
B)  fewer classical music fans today listen to
music created by young composers.
C)  the artistic quality of classical music concerts
had been on the decline for years.
D)  classical music concerts designed for younger
audiences have been unpopular.

_____ 2.  Unlike the author of Passage 1, the author of
Passage 2:

A)  makes the case that attendance at classical
music concerts is likely to increase.
B)  criticizes composers from the recent past for
writing music that was not adventurous.
C)  points out that people today are less musically
knowledgeable.
D)  addresses causes for a decline in interest in
classical music.

**MAIN IDEAS:**

A: _____

B: _____

CONTINUE

*Course C: Homework 5*

*A-List Education*

# Reading: Double Passage 2

**Passage 1**

Amid the general concern over climate change, there has been less focus on rainforest deforestation. Deforestation, especially in the Amazon, is of course, a *Line* significant driver of global warming: the ldeoss of trees, 5 which consume carbon dioxide, leads to greater amounts of carbon in the air, leading in turn to more heat being trapped in Earth's lower atmosphere.

However, other serious dangers arise from the indiscriminate slash-and-burn approach that continues 10 to be used in the Amazon by loggers and others. The indigenous people have been treated roughly, at times brutally, as their homelands have been destroyed or made uninhabitable. The number of plant and animal species continues to decline at a rate estimated at 50,000 15 species annually. Deforestation also typically leads to soil erosion, and once fertile areas turn into wasteland.

**Passage 2**

A number of steps have been taken to curb the serious environmental dangers associated with defor-estation. One of the most common-sense approaches 20 involves a stricter monitoring of forest loss. Arial photographs can be studied by individuals who do not possess advanced training. Satellite images of so-called hot spots, areas most susceptible to rapid loss, can be analyzed. These methods can be used to track regrowth 25 as well as forest loss.

Another important advance is the development of new farming methods that minimize the amount of deforested land needed by small local farmers by showing them how to increase crop yield. A particularly 30 inventive method for accomplishing this is the creation of food forests that replicate natural forests. These agroforestal systems have proved successful at reducing dependence on fossil fuels and chemicals and improving the quality of the local soil and water. More importantly, 35 this is both a pragmatic and an ethical way to keep in mind the rights of the people who have lived in the forest all their lives.

**MAIN IDEAS:**

A: _____

B: _____

____ 3. Both passages mention the people who have always lived in the rainforest, but only Passage 2:

A) involves them in ways to remedy the problem of deforestation.
B) explains how they have helped formulate ways to alleviate the problem of deforestation.
C) states that they have been treated brutally at times in the past.
D) acknowledges that there has been a lessening of habitat loss due to deforestation in recent years.

____ 4. It can be inferred from the passage that the author of Passage 2 would most likely:

A) feel that the author of Passage 1 has overstated the threat posed by deforestation.
B) strongly agree with the concerns expressed by the author of Passage 1.
C) argue that the solutions proposed by the author of Passage 1 are impractical.
D) point out that climate change is only one threat posed by deforestation.

CONTINUE

# Reading: Double Passage 3

**Passage 1**

In July of 2011, the General Assembly of the United Nations decided to ask member nations to determine the happiness of their people by simply asking them. The idea *Line* was to see not just how people felt about their lives, but 5 also what aspects of their nations' structure and services added to their happiness or took from it.

The result was the World Happiness Report, which is revised annually. Besides ranking countries based on their World Happiness Index, the report includes analyses of 10 how individual well-being is tied to a nation's progress. Ethics, mental illness, and many other topics are discussed in some depth. Six variables have been identified as being strongly associated with happiness: gross domestic product (GDP) per capita, social support, healthy life 15 expectancy, freedom to make life choices, generosity, and perceived corruption. One country, Bhutan, has gone so far as to make *gross national happiness* its main development indicator.

**Passage 2**

The annual World Happiness Report published by the 20 UN's Sustainable Development Solutions Network is meant to provide insights into how a nation's culture, economy, and governmental structure contributes to its citizens' happiness or, sad to say, their misery. With this knowledge in hand, leaders can then institute policy 25 changes so as to improve lives.

That's the theory anyway. The report has yet to deliver any surprises. As expected, Western European countries, with their well-fed, well-educated, well-protected citizens generally top the charts. Similar 30 countries such as New Zealand and the U.S. also score well, usually in the top 15 out of more than 150 countries. This is not terribly useful information to poorer countries who strive for greater happiness.

**MAIN IDEAS:**

A: _____

B: _____

5. The author of Passage 2, unlike the author of Passage 1, uses a tone that is sometimes

A) optimistic
B) humorous
C) skeptical
D) morose

6. Which of the following best describes a difference between the two passages?

A) Passage 1 focuses on the content of the report, while Passage 2 focuses on the purpose of the report.
B) Passage 1 focuses on the results of the report, while Passage 2 focuses on the format of the report.
C) Passage 1 focuses on changes to the report since its inception, while Passage 2 focuses on the report's creation.
D) Passage 1 provides data about individual nations that took part in the index, while Passage 2 provides data regarding the ranking of the nations in the index.

**CONTINUE** ➡

# Math: Graphing Functions

_____ 7. What is the slope of the line that passes through the points $(1, 2)$ and $(3, 8)$ ?

    A)   $-3$
    B)   $-1/3$
    C)   $1/3$
    D)   $3$

_____ 8. What is the slope of the line that passes through the points $(-6, 4)$ and $(1, -3)$ ?

    A)   $-7/6$
    B)   $-6/7$
    C)   $-1$
    D)   $1$

_____ 9. What is the $y$-intercept of the line that passes through the points $(1, -1)$ and $(5, 7)$ ?

    A)   $-3$
    B)   $-2$
    C)   $-1$
    D)   $1$

_____ 10. What is the $x$-intercept of the line that passes through the points $(1, -1)$ and $(5, 7)$ ?

    A)   $1/2$
    B)   $3/2$
    C)   $5/2$
    D)   $7/2$

_____ 11. The equation of line $\ell$ is $y = 3x + 7$. If line $k$ is perpendicular to line $\ell$, what is the slope of line $k$?

    A)   $-3$
    B)   $-1/3$
    C)   $1/3$
    D)   $3/7$

_____ 12. The equation of line $\ell$ is $y = 3x - 1$. If line $m$ is the reflection of line $\ell$ across the $x$-axis, what is the slope of line $m$?

    A)   $-3$
    B)   $-1/3$
    C)   $-1$
    D)   $1/3$

_____ 13. The equation of line $\ell$ is $y = -2x + 3$. If line $k$ is parallel to line $\ell$ and passes through the point $(3,5)$, what is the $y$-intercept of line $k$?

    A)   $8$
    B)   $9$
    C)   $10$
    D)   $11$

CONTINUE ▶

_____ **14.** Which of the following could be the graph of

$$y = -\frac{1}{2}x + 2 \text{ ?}$$

A)

B)

C)

D)

_____ **16.** Let the function $f$ be defined by

$f(x) = ax^2 + bx + c$ where $a$, $b$, and $c$ are constants. If $a < 0$ and $c > 0$, then which of the following could be the graph of $f$?

A)

B)

C)

D)

_____ **15.** Which of the following could be the graph of
$y = 2x - 3$ ?

A)

B)

C)

D)

**STOP**

# Homework 6

## Writing: Redundancy 1

_____ 1. <u>Every year, our</u> glee club's annual charity benefit raises money to fund music education in poor countries around the world.

    1. A) NO CHANGE
        B) Once a year, our
        C) Our
        D) As a yearly charity event, our

_____ 2. Last year my family took a trip to the Netherlands, and I was amazed by the clean public <u>parks there that were so neat.</u>

    2. A) NO CHANGE
        B) parks there in the Netherlands.
        C) tidily there in the Netherlands.
        D) parks.

_____ 3. Owen and Logan are pooling their money to buy an advanced digital camera, so they can film the movie script that <u>Owen wrote.</u>

    3. A) NO CHANGE
        B) he wrote.
        C) Owen wrote for a movie.
        D) was written by him for them to film.

_____ 4. Isabel knew that she shouldn't open the <u>strange, rumbling box that was making noise</u> in the corner of her grandparent's attic.

    4. A) NO CHANGE
        B) odd, rumbling box that was strange
        C) strange, rumbling box
        D) odd and strange box

_____ 5. Pyramids can be found around the world. They were often built by slaves and usually served as religious <u>buildings across the globe.</u>

    5. A) NO CHANGE
        B) buildings globally.
        C) buildings.
        D) structures anywhere in the world.

CONTINUE ➡

# Writing: Redundancy 2

_____ **6.** Stringed instruments played by hand have existed for thousands of years, but the first instruments with recognizable similarities to modern guitars were created in Spain in the 13th century. <u>They have traits in common with modern guitars.</u>

**6.** A) NO CHANGE
B) These Spanish instruments share a number of traits with modern guitars.
C) Modern guitars have a number of similarities to them.
D) DELETE the underlined portion.

_____ **7.** Because his car broke down, all week my friend has found himself in the <u>unfortunate and luckless position</u> of needing to ask his older brother for a ride to work.

**7.** A) NO CHANGE
B) unfortunate position
C) unlucky position for the whole week
D) lucklessly unfortunate position

_____ **8.** Our local tennis <u>club, which serves the nearby area,</u> is planning a tournament for Labor Day weekend.

**8.** A) NO CHANGE
B) club
C) club of tennis players
D) club, which plays tennis,

_____ **9.** Victoria eased past the old marble statue and <u>carefully avoided touching its marble form with great care</u> to prevent it from collapsing.

**9.** A) NO CHANGE
B) with great care avoided touching or contacting it
C) carefully avoided touching it
D) using great care avoided any contact so as not to touch the statue

_____ **10.** Sierra was very proud of her encyclopedic knowledge of mid-nineties television shows and was <u>happy</u> to demonstrate it at parties.

**10.** A) NO CHANGE
B) happy and amicable
C) happy to show and
D) DELETE the underlined portion.

# Writing: Transitions 1

_____ 11. Robert the Bald defeated Prince Ethelrood at the Battle of the Three Rivers. He was, <u>however,</u> able to the prince's throne by right of conquest.

11. A) NO CHANGE
    B) nevertheless,
    C) therefore,
    D) previously,

_____ 12. When it comes to running the restaurant, my boss micromanages us way too much. <u>Nevertheless,</u> he makes us account for where every lemon slice goes, and he refuses to let anyone else fold the napkins.

12. A) NO CHANGE
    B) On the other hand,
    C) For example,
    D) Surprisingly,

_____ 13. The Brontë sisters—Charlotte, Emily, and Anne—may very well make up the most talented family of writers in human history. <u>All three</u> enjoyed success as poets and novelists.

13. A) NO CHANGE
    B) However, all three
    C) All three, in contrast,
    D) Therefore, all three

_____ 14. <u>Because</u> the Berlin Wall was brought down more than 25 years ago, differences between the two halves of the city remain.

14. A) NO CHANGE
    B) Although
    C) Before
    D) If

_____ 15. The research team believes there may be a link between low rainfall and the migration routes of geese. <u>For example,</u> they will tag several specimens to track whether the geese appear in areas that have recently experienced drought.

15. A) NO CHANGE
    B) Nevertheless,
    C) Coincidentally,
    D) For this reason,

CONTINUE →

# Writing: Transitions 2

_____ **16.** To celebrate the 4th of July, the city council has planned a giant parade and a million-dollar fireworks spectacle. The whole plan may be in jeopardy, <u>additionally,</u> if this torrential rain refuses to stop.

**16.** A) NO CHANGE
B) therefore,
C) for instance,
D) however,

_____ **17.** Because there is disagreement about what level of soccer counts as "professional", it is difficult to determine the leading scorer of all time. <u>Conversely,</u> some sources name Pelé as having the most goals while others believe it to be Josef Bican.

**17.** A) NO CHANGE
B) On the other hand,
C) Consequently,
D) At that time,

_____ **18.** *Turritopsis dohrnii* is a species of jellyfish that is able to revert from its adult state back to an immature polyp at any time. <u>In light of this ability,</u> the species is called the "immortal jellyfish."

**18.** A) NO CHANGE
B) Despite this talent,
C) That is because
D) Surprisingly, this means

_____ **19.** Theories about the true authorship of Shakespeare's plays are plentiful. In the academic community, <u>therefore,</u> proposed alternative authors are rarely taken seriously, as there is no concrete evidence to suggest any of them wrote the plays.

**19.** A) NO CHANGE
B) as one example,
C) similarly,
D) however,

_____ **20.** At the annual harvest festival, the villagers would bring all their crops to the square to be judged, <u>while</u> those chosen as the finest would be brought to the temple at the top of the mountain.

**20.** A) NO CHANGE
B) although
C) during which
D) after which

CONTINUE

**Name:** _____ **Date:** _____

# Math: Technique Review

**DIRECTIONS: You must use an SAT math technique** on each of the following questions. You must indicate which technique you used—either **Plug In** or **Backsolve**—and show your work.

_____ 21. Alvin, Barney, and Cedric made a total of 18 sandwiches to bring to a picnic. Alvin made 2 more sandwiches than Barney made, and Cedric made 3 times as many as Alvin. How many sandwiches did Barney make?

    A)    2
    B)    4
    C)    6
    D)    10

_____ 22. **Technique used:**

    A)   Plug In
    B)   Backsolve

_____ 23. If Arthur was $y$ years old exactly 3 years ago, how old will he be in exactly $x$ years?

    A)   $x + y$
    B)   $x + y - 3$
    C)   $x - y - 3$
    D)   $x + y + 3$

_____ 24. **Technique used:**

    A)   Plug In
    B)   Backsolve

_____ 25. The high road to Scotland is 180 miles longer than the low road. When Jocelyn goes to Scotland by the high road and returns along the low road, the round trip is 1,060 miles. How many miles is the high road?

    A)   350
    B)   440
    C)   530
    D)   620

_____ 26. **Technique used:**

    A)   Plug In
    B)   Backsolve

_____ 27. If $a$, $b$, and $c$ are consecutive even integers such that $a < b < c$, which of the following is equal to $a^2 + b^2 + c^2$?

    A)   $3b^2 + 2$
    B)   $3b^2 + 6$
    C)   $3b^2 + 8$
    D)   $3b^2 + 6b + 5$

_____ 28. **Technique used:**

    A)   Plug In
    B)   Backsolve

_____ 29. It takes Donna 4 minutes to grade an essay, and it takes Clay 6 minutes to grade an essay. If they both start working at the same time, how many minutes will it take them to grade 20 total essays?

    A)    40
    B)    48
    C)    72
    D)    100

_____ 30. **Technique used:**

    A)   Plug In
    B)   Backsolve

## STOP

# Course D

3 hr 30 hr

# Homework 1

## Reading: Passage 1

Most people use the word "hobo" as little more than a derogatory term for the homeless, deriding them as lazy bums who spend their days idly wandering the country. However, the word properly refers to an
*Line*
5   itinerant worker. Far from lazy, hobos travel hundreds of miles looking for any work they can find. When jobs were especially scarce during the Great Depression several hundred thousand hobos traveled from town to town, hitching rides in railway freight cars and carrying
10   only the bare essentials on their backs. As their numbers increased, hobo culture became more organized, developing ways to communicate with each other to keep safe. These included homemade travel books and a system of written symbols to inform other hobos
15   whether nearby houses were friendly or hostile. Today, hobos even have their own union and an annual convention in Britt, Iowa, home of the National Hobo Museum.

**MAIN IDEA:** _____

_____

_____ 1. In context, the author includes lines 1-4 ("Most… country") in order to

**ANTICIPATION:** _____

_____

A)  present a common opinion the author will refute
B)  demonstrate the proper connotation of a word
C)  disparage the indolence of the hobo lifestyle
D)  detail the history of itinerant workers in the U.S.

_____ 2. The "books" (line 13) and the "system" (line 14) are given as examples of

**ANTICIPATION:** _____

_____

A)  objects that can be seen in the National Hobo Museum
B)  the dangers that hobos can encounter on the road
C)  methods hobos use for interacting with their peers
D)  tools needed to perform a typical job that a hobo finds

CONTINUE ➡

# Reading: Passage 2

Americans are spoiled by the mutual intelligibility of the regional variations of their language. The differences between dialects within the country are trivial, such as whether a carbonated beverage is called "soda" or "pop" or whether "caramel" should be pronounced with two syllables or three. When compared with other languages, American English shows astonishing little variation. In Germany, for example, there are over a dozen distinct Germanic languages spoken, from Alemannic to Westphalian, some of which have deep grammatical differences beyond simple vocabulary or phonology. The difference can be starker with German spoken in other countries: the "German" spoken in Switzerland is practically incomprehensible to one who speaks only Standard German. When Americans travel in America, other people may sound funny, but they understand each other. If a German strays too far from home, the people around him might as well be speaking Latin.

*Line 5*

*10*

*15*

**MAIN IDEA:** _____

_____

_____ **3.** The author says Americans are "spoiled" (line 1) because they

**ANTICIPATION:** _____

_____

A) struggle to learn many different varieties of American English
B) use different words for common things than people from other parts of the country
C) have little difficulty understanding each other compared with people in other countries
D) speak a language that has no variation across the country

_____ **4.** In line 19, "Latin" serves as an example of a language that

**ANTICIPATION:** _____

_____

A) has significant dialectical variation
B) is a dialect spoken within Germany
C) only varies in simple vocabulary and phonology
D) is so foreign that it is incomprehensible

**CONTINUE**

# Reading: Passage 3

George Balanchine is rightly remembered as one of the greatest choreographers of our time, but his muses, the women who inspired him, are just as deserving of
Line acclaim. He seemingly was never without a muse, from
5 Vera Zorina in Broadway musicals and Hollywood films, to prima ballerina Maria Tallchief in *The Nutcracker* and *Swan Lake*, to Suzanne Farrell in *Meditation* and *Don Quixote*. These women did not simply perform his work: the work itself would not exist
10 without them. Unlike a painter or a writer, a choreographer like Balanchine is only one of many contributors to an artwork, and his muses can actively shape the result. The dancers are directed by his designs, but his designs are also transformed by their dancing.
15 Each of Balanchine's works merged his artistic vision with a different dancer's soul and spirit.

**MAIN IDEA:** _____

_____

_____ **5.** The author of the passage argues that Balanchine's "muses" (line 2)

**ANTICIPATION:** _____

_____

A) believed they did not get recognition for their contributions
B) deserve more credit than Balanchine for the value of his work
C) significantly contributed to Balanchine's work
D) were not sufficiently appreciated by Balanchine

_____ **6.** In lines 10-13 ("Unlike … the result") the author suggests

**ANTICIPATION:** _____

_____

A) painters and writers do not generally have muses
B) Balanchine was unhappy about his lack of control over his work
C) female painters and writers have fewer opportunities than female dancers
D) some artists have greater effect on their own work than Balanchine had

CONTINUE ➡

# Math: Plug In

**DIRECTIONS: You must use Plug In** on each of the following questions. Write your answer in the space before the question number.

_____ 7.  Alan has $x$ chocolate bars and gets 10 more bars. He gives away half of his chocolate, and then gets another 10 bars. In terms of $x$, how many chocolate bars does Alan now have?

A)  $x + 15$
B)  $x + 20$
C)  $\dfrac{x}{2}$
D)  $\dfrac{x}{2} + 15$

_____ 8.  If $a$ is 5 less than twice $b$, which of the following gives $b$ in terms of $a$?

A)  $2a - 5$
B)  $5 + 2a$
C)  $\dfrac{5 - a}{2}$
D)  $\dfrac{a + 5}{2}$

_____ 9.  Stewart's car can hold a maximum of $g$ gallons in its gas tank, and gas costs $c$ dollars per gallon. If the car currently has 2 gallons of gas in the tank, what is the cost, in dollars, to fill up the rest of the tank?

A)  $cg - 2$
B)  $cg - 2c$
C)  $cg - 2g$
D)  $g - 2c$

_____ 10.  In a series of three numbers, the second number is 3 less than the first, and the third is three times the second. If the first number is $x$, how much greater than the second number is the third number?

A)  $2x - 6$
B)  $2x - 9$
C)  $2x - 12$
D)  $3x - 3$

_____ 11.  Olivia earns a commission of 15 percent of the price of every boat she sells. Which of the following gives the amount of her commission, in dollars, if she sells $x$ boats that each cost $y$ dollars?

A)  $15xy$
B)  $1500xy$
C)  $\dfrac{3xy}{20}$
D)  $\dfrac{3y}{20x}$

**STOP**

# Homework 2

## Writing: Verbs 1

_____ 1. My best friend, who enjoys making music and plays several instruments, <u>plan</u> to visit Maine this winter and write songs in a cabin.

1. A) NO CHANGE
   B) have planned
   C) are planning
   D) plans

_____ 2. When they worked together at the library, Naomi and Nicholas <u>hunt</u> through the aisles for books with ridiculous names.

2. A) NO CHANGE
   B) will hunt
   C) would hunt
   D) are hunting

_____ 3. It looks like our hike might be cut short because a swarm of angry bees <u>have blocked</u> the trail ahead.

3. A) NO CHANGE
   B) is blocking
   C) would block
   D) are blocking

_____ 4. In 1965, Soviet cosmonaut Alexey Leonov <u>will perform</u> the first extra-vehicular space walk in human history.

4. A) NO CHANGE
   B) performs
   C) performed
   D) has performed

_____ 5. The dulcet tones of the piano that had been drifting across the restaurant to the table where Danny waited for his date <u>were</u> suddenly drowned out by the sound of a blender running in the kitchen.

5. A) NO CHANGE
   B) has been
   C) was
   D) is

CONTINUE ➡

# Writing: Verbs 2

_____ **6.** In Professor Tomlin's lab, a team of undergraduate students <u>have found</u> a way to "listen" to space by monitoring radio waves as they travel through the cosmic void.

**6.** A) NO CHANGE
B) are finding
C) find
D) has found

_____ **7.** Past the stone monument that marks the end of the beach, <u>lies</u> two tide pools that glitter beautifully in the moonlight.

**7.** A) NO CHANGE
B) lie
C) has lied
D) is

_____ **8.** Next spring, the Emergency Response Team created by the previous mayor <u>has been</u> replaced by a smaller Emergency Dispatch Service that will direct existing resources to respond to crises.

**8.** A) NO CHANGE
B) was
C) is
D) will be

_____ **9.** The requests that Joanna's employees made— on a number of topics but most notably for more vacation time—<u>were</u> reasonable, so she happily changed her policies.

**9.** A) NO CHANGE
B) would be
C) was
D) is

_____ **10.** Because it <u>had been containing</u> private details about his own life and family, Eugene O'Neill's masterpiece _A Long Day's Journey Into Night_ was not published until after his death.

**10.** A) NO CHANGE
B) contained
C) will contain
D) has contained

**CONTINUE**

# Writing: Pronouns 1

_____ **11.** All the apartments in the new buildings have a new washing machine for the convenience of <u>it's</u> occupants.

**11.** A) NO CHANGE
    B) their
    C) its
    D) there

_____ **12.** I thought this coat looked great on me at the store, but when I got home I found that <u>it's</u> not exactly the color I expected.

**12.** A) NO CHANGE
    B) its
    C) its'
    D) they're

_____ **13.** Ian loved the look of his new phone, but disliked <u>its'</u> lack of features.

**13.** A) NO CHANGE
    B) their
    C) its
    D) it's

_____ **14.** Every meeting of the Iowa Misanthrope Club ends with a vote for a new chairperson, <u>whom</u> would be forced to host the next meeting.

**14.** A) NO CHANGE
    B) who
    C) which
    D) whose

_____ **15.** If one wishes to build a successful business, <u>they</u> should carefully consider how to stand out from competing ventures.

**15.** A) NO CHANGE
    B) we
    C) you
    D) one

CONTINUE →

# Writing: Pronouns 2

_____ **16.** The school's new policy allows students to easily obtain a copy of <u>their</u> attendance or academic records at any point during the year.

**16.**
A) NO CHANGE
B) his or her
C) they're
D) your

_____ **17.** Paul and Olivia liked how <u>they're</u> new back yard opened up directly to a meadow with a tiny stream.

**17.**
A) NO CHANGE
B) its
C) there
D) their

_____ **18.** The hippopotamus, despite having an innocuous appearance, is actually extremely dangerous and can kill with <u>their</u> powerful bite.

**18.**
A) NO CHANGE
B) they're
C) its
D) it's

_____ **19.** Scientists at NASA are planning a mission to bring an asteroid into lunar orbit so <u>they</u> can be studied more easily by astronauts.

**19.**
A) NO CHANGE
B) it
C) which
D) them

_____ **20.** After the conclusion of the piano recital, the teacher asked <u>my friend and I</u> to play a duet together as the audience left the auditorium.

**20.**
A) NO CHANGE
B) my friend and me
C) I and my friend
D) my friend and myself

CONTINUE →

# Math: Backsolve

**DIRECTIONS: You must use Backsolve** on each of the following questions. Write your answer in the space before the question number.

_____ **21.** Tree X is 23 inches tall and tree Y is 73 inches tall. Tree X grows 5 inches a year and tree Y grows 3 inches a year. In how many years will tree X be the same height as tree Y?

    A) 10
    B) 15
    C) 25
    D) 30

$$a + b = 17$$
$$b + c = 35$$
$$a + c = 28$$

_____ **24.** In the system of equations above, what is the value of $a$?

    A) 5
    B) 10
    C) 12
    D) 24

_____ **22.** At a movie theater, small drinks cost $3 each and large drinks cost $5 each. The theater sells 100 total drinks for a total of $380. How many small drinks were sold?

    A) 45
    B) 50
    C) 55
    D) 60

_____ **25.** Molly has 36 more red shirts than blue shirts. Half the number of red shirts equals twice the number of blue shirts. How many blue shirts does she have?

    A) 9
    B) 12
    C) 24
    D) 36

$$B(d) = 2d^2 + 10$$

_____ **23.** The function $B$, defined above, models the number of new bees born in a beehive after $d$ days. According to this model, how many days would it take for the colony to gain 108 new bees?

    A) 4
    B) 5
    C) 6
    D) 7

CONTINUE ➜

# Math: Fundamentals Review

_____ 26. If $\dfrac{a}{2} \times \dfrac{1}{8} = \dfrac{\frac{3}{4}}{6}$ , then $a = ?$

    A) 2
    B) 3
    C) 4
    D) 6

_____ 27. What is the remainder when 52 is divided by 3?

    A) 0
    B) 1
    C) 2
    D) 3

_____ 28. A recipe calls for 3 cups of flour for every 5 cups of sugar. If Bill uses 15 cups of flour, how many cups of sugar should he use?

    A) 10
    B) 15
    C) 20
    D) 25

_____ 29. A certain park contains only maple and elm trees in a ratio of 2 to 3, respectively. If there are a total of 40 trees, how many elm trees are there in the park?

    A) 16
    B) 18
    C) 20
    D) 24

_____ 30. What percent of 40 is 8?

    A) 5
    B) 10
    C) 20
    D) 30

_____ 31. 9 is 15 percent of what number?

    A) 60
    B) 70
    C) 75
    D) 80

_____ 32. Joe made 160 dollars last week and 180 dollars this week. What was the percent increase in his pay?

    A) 10
    B) 12.5
    C) 15
    D) 17.5

_____ 33. $x^3 \left( x^2 \right)^5 = ?$

    A) $x^5$
    B) $x^7$
    C) $x^{10}$
    D) $x^{13}$

_____ 34. If $d^3 \times d^4 = d^p$ and $\dfrac{d^{12}}{d^6} = d^q$ , what is $p + q$ ?

    A) 1
    B) 6
    C) 7
    D) 13

_____ 35. If $|x - 6| = 23$, which of the following gives all possible values of $x$?

    A) $-29$
    B) $-17$
    C) $-17$ and 29
    D) 17 and $-29$

**STOP**

Name: _____ Date: _____

# Homework 3

## Reading: Explicit Questions 1

*Gravitational waves* are changes in the curvature of space-time, moving at light-speed, that are initiated by accelerating bodies found within binary star systems.
*Line* These bodies can be neutron stars, white dwarf stars, or
5 black holes. When, for example, binary neutron stars orbit close to each other, the extremely large acceleration of their masses form gravitational waves. An observer would notice rhythmic (wave-like) distortions in local space-time. Distances between
10 objects would fluctuate with the frequency of the wave.

So do these waves actually affect Earth? The short answer is yes, but because of the astronomical distances involved, the effect is so minuscule that only the most sensitive devices can measure the effect. The first
15 observation of a gravitational wave was made on September 14th, 2015. Two black holes, each about 30 times more massive than our sun, had spiraled and merged, creating an unimaginably powerful wave that finally reached us after traveling through a billion light
20 years of space. By the time it got here, it was detected by a device whose 4-kilometer arm changed in length by the unimaginably small distance of ten-thousandths of the width of a proton.

MAIN IDEA: _____

_____

_____ 1. According to the passage, the gravitational wave that scientists were first able to observe was:

ANTICIPATION: _____

_____

A) created by an event that took place in 2015.
B) found within the orbit of neutron stars.
C) created through the interactions of two black holes.
D) measured to be approximately 4-kilometers long.

_____ 2. The passage states that the large acceleration of massive objects in space:

ANTICIPATION: _____

_____

A) can alter the way that space and time appear to behave.
B) can cause binary star systems to orbit each other more closely.
C) typically produce fluctuations in local space-time conditions that are observable from Earth.
D) are responses to curvatures in space-time.

CONTINUE →

# Reading: Vocab-in-context Questions 1

Donald looked at Tim Capulsky, slumped in front of the television in his hotel room watching the local news. He eyed this man who was his friend, client, and
Line very possibly the next senator of New Jersey, and was
5 glad to see him inert for a change. It was an exhausting day, and tomorrow wouldn't be much better. Donald had the urge to turn off the TV and carry him to his bed and tuck him in. He chuckled softly at the image and Capulsky turned around but said nothing. Once the
10 program turned from politics to gossip, the candidate stretched and shut the TV off. He looked at his friend.

"Don't worry. I'm happy. May not look it right now, but I'm happy. I'm definitely pleased with all you've been doing. Sometimes I want to tell the folks,
15 'Hey, if you like me, you'll really like the guy whose doing most of the heavy lifting—the brains of the outfit' and then dragging you to the podium."

"Don't do that."

They both smiled almost the exact same smile. An
20 unwelcome rapping at the door broke the moment and Capulsky put a finger to his lips. He made a head-on-pillow gesture and backed his way into his bedroom, saluting his good night. Donald nodded his approval and readied his own excuse as he approached the door.

**MAIN IDEA:** _____

_____

_____ **3.** Which of the following is closest to the meaning of *inert* as it is used in line 5?

**ANTICIPATION:** _____

_____

A) motionless
B) asleep
C) inoperative
D) exhausted

_____ **4.** Which of the following is closest to the meaning of *readied* as it is used in line 24?

**ANTICIPATION:** _____

_____

A) began
B) remembered
C) prepared
D) embellished

**CONTINUE**

# Reading: Main Idea Questions 1

Vegetarianism in on the rise in virtually all demographic groups in the United States and in much of the rest of the world. Even more impressive is the rate
*Line* of increase in the percentage of the U.S. population that
5 has substantially cut back on their animal product intake. These changes are not fads: analysts of every segment of the food industry agree that the American diet has irrevocably altered.

The reasons for this are many and overlapping.
10 Nutrition and animal well-being, not surprisingly, are the most often cited, but increasingly, recent converts to vegetarianism mention cost, weight loss, food safety, and religious proscriptions as motivating factors. Interestingly, the reason most often given by *non-*
15 *vegetarians* for why they choose to remain meat-eaters—taste—also plays a role in the decision of others to forego animal products. In the last ten years, food manufacturers have become more skilled at producing easy-to-prepare vegetarian items that simply taste
20 delicious.

**MAIN IDEA:** _____

_____

_____ **5.** The primary function of the first paragraph is to:

**ANTICIPATION:** _____

_____

A) briefly describe the how the food industry tracks vegetarianism.
B) explain that the United States has started a worldwide rise in vegetarianism.
C) show that the author approves in the rise in vegetarianism.
D) identify the trend that people in the United States eat less meat and will continue to do so.

_____ **6.** The main purpose of the second paragraph is to:

**ANTICIPATION:** _____

_____

A) give arguments in favor of the changes discussed in the first paragraph.
B) present an overview of a range of recent changes that have taken place in the American diet.
C) discuss changes in the manufacturing process of vegetarian meals.
D) provide possible explanations for the increase in vegetarianism.

CONTINUE

# Reading: Inferential Questions 1

The sight of the mimic octopus living up to its name is one of the most extraordinary in all of nature. Other animals have impressive abilities to change their appearance to resemble different animals or blend in with their surroundings, as do all species of octopus to some extent, but *Thaumoctopus mimicus* is, as far we know, unsurpassed in the range of its mimicry. It is believed to be able to imitate fifteen other local marine organisms.

*Line 5*

It is not just the general shape and coloring of an animal that this octopus imitates. When, for example, it mimics a flounder or jellyfish, it moves in a manner uncannily like these creatures. Perhaps not surprisingly, given its relative vulnerability, the mimic octopus is particularly adept at taking on the appearance of poisonous or venomous animals. It can, for example, mimic a poisonous sea snake by burying all but two of its legs in the ocean floor, and then extending these two out straight.

*10*

*15*

**MAIN IDEA:** _____

_____

_____ 7. It can reasonably be inferred from the passage that the mimic octopus lacks the ability to:

**ANTICIPATION:** _____

_____

A) use venom to defend itself.
B) imitate animals that prey upon it.
C) mimic plant life.
D) bury itself completely in the ocean floor.

_____ 8. It can be inferred from paragraph 1 that other species of octopus besides the mimic octopus can:

**ANTICIPATION:** _____

_____

A) change their appearance in less impressive ways than the mimic octopus.
B) imitate the shape and coloring of the mimic octopus.
C) move or behave like the organisms they are mimicking.
D) imitate up to fifteen other local marine organisms.

CONTINUE ➤

# Math: Algebra

_____ **9.** If $3x + 5 = 17$, $x = ?$

A) 3
B) 4
C) 5
D) 6

_____ **10.** If $5x - 13 = 32$, $x = ?$

A) 9
B) 10
C) 11
D) 12

_____ **11.** If $4x - 21 = 56 - 3x$, $x = ?$

A) 3
B) 5
C) 9
D) 11

_____ **12.** If $\dfrac{3x+8}{2} = 16$, $x = ?$

A) 5
B) 6
C) 7
D) 8

_____ **13.** If $3(2x - 9) = 15$, $x = ?$

A) 1
B) 4
C) 5
D) 7

_____ **14.** If $\sqrt{x-9} = 2$, $x = ?$

A) −3
B) 3
C) 13
D) 23

_____ **15.** If $(x - 5)(x + 6) = x^2$, $x = ?$

A) 15
B) 20
C) 25
D) 30

_____ **16.** $4y + 5x + 14 = 2y + 7x + 20$, what is $y$ in terms of $x$?

A) $y = x - 3$
B) $y = x + 3$
C) $y = 2x + 4$
D) $y = 2x + 6$

$$2a + b = 9$$
$$3b + c = 25$$
$$2a + 3c = 14$$

_____ **17.** Given the system of equations above, what is the value of $a + b + c$?

A) 8
B) 10
C) 12
D) 16

_____ **18.** If $x + y = 10$ and $x^2 - y^2 = 60$, what is the value of $x - y$?

A) 6
B) 8
C) 10
D) 12

# STOP

# Homework 4

## Writing: Fragments 1

_____ 1. Waffles, though primarily served at breakfast in America, <u>but eaten</u> throughout the day in Belgium.

1. A) NO CHANGE
   B) eaten
   C) are eaten
   D) eating

_____ 2. The launch of the new <u>website, already delayed</u> three weeks when the developers were forced to postpone it indefinitely.

2. A) NO CHANGE
   B) website; it was already delayed
   C) website was already delayed
   D) website, which was already delayed

_____ 3. Nepal's national <u>flag, which is the world's only non-rectangular national flag and also</u> the only flag that is taller than it is wide.

3. A) NO CHANGE
   B) flag, which is the world's only non-rectangular national flag and which is
   C) flag, the world's only non-rectangular national flag, as well as
   D) flag is the world's only non-rectangular national flag and also

_____ 4. The northern cardinal, <u>one of the most common birds in North America, and also</u> the official bird of seven different U.S. states.

4. A) NO CHANGE
   B) one of the most common birds in North America, is
   C) which is one of the most common birds in North America and
   D) which is one of the most common birds in North America and is

_____ 5. Harry Beck's landmark 1931 map of the London Underground rail <u>system depicting</u> train lines only in straight lines with orthogonal angles, with no reference to actual geography or topology.

5. A) NO CHANGE
   B) system depicted
   C) system that depicted
   D) system; it depicted

CONTINUE ➡

Name: _____ Date: _____

# **Writing: Fragments 2**

_____ **6.** Dwayne Johnson, also known as The <u>Rock, who has</u> made a skillful transition from professional wrestler to Hollywood actor.

**6.** A) NO CHANGE
   B) Rock, having
   C) Rock, and who has
   D) Rock, has

_____ **7.** If the school's administrators are serious about increasing <u>enrollment. They</u> should take a hard look at where they're spending their money.

**7.** A) NO CHANGE
   B) enrollment, they
   C) enrollment; they
   D) enrollment,

_____ **8.** In Myanmar, the military <u>having excluded Aung San Suu Kyi,</u> the leader of the country's democratic movement, from holding the office of president.

**8.** A) NO CHANGE
   B) has excluded Aung San Suu Kyi,
   C) having excluded Aung San Suu Kyi, who is
   D) excluding Aung San Suu Kyi,

_____ **9.** Even though the forecast didn't call for <u>rain, Mary still packed</u> an umbrella for her vacation, knowing that the local climate was highly unpredictable.

**9.** A) NO CHANGE
   B) rain. Mary still packed
   C) rain, Mary still packing
   D) rain, but Mary still packed

_____ **10.** Descending deeper and deeper into the murky depths, Jordan Summers, the leader of the scuba diving tour, <u>while keeping</u> a close eye on the less experienced divers in her group.

**10.** A) NO CHANGE
   B) keeping
   C) kept
   D) who kept

CONTINUE

# Writing: Run-Ons 1

_____ 11. Andrew Johnson was impeached by the House of Representatives in <u>1868, then he was acquitted</u> in the Senate by one vote, allowing him to continue his term as President of the United States.

11. A) NO CHANGE
    B) 1868, he was acquitted
    C) 1868; acquitted
    D) 1868; however, he was acquitted

_____ 12. Despite their image as a quintessentially American fruit, apples were first cultivated in Kazakhstan in central Asia, <u>China is the largest apple producer today</u>.

12. A) NO CHANGE
    B) China produces apples in the largest number today
    C) and China is the largest apple producer today
    D) today it is China that produces the most apples

_____ 13. It had been twenty years since Shelly had visited her <u>hometown, she feared</u> what it had become in the time she was gone.

13. A) NO CHANGE
    B) hometown; she being afraid of
    C) hometown, and she feared
    D) hometown, therefore she feared

_____ 14. <u>Jeff initially did not feel prepared for the test,</u> he had no trouble with any of the questions once it started.

14. A) NO CHANGE
    B) Jeff's initial feeling was that he was not prepared for the test
    C) Initially, Jeff felt that he was not prepared for the test
    D) Although Jeff initially did not feel prepared for the test

_____ 15. Most people consider George Washington to be America's first President, but some argue it was technically John <u>Hanson, he was President of the Continental Congress</u> under the Articles of Confederation from 1781 to 1782.

15. A) NO CHANGE
    B) Hanson, who was President of the Continental Congress
    C) Hanson, the President of the Continental Congress was
    D) Hanson; President of the Continental Congress

CONTINUE ➡

# Writing: Run-Ons 2

_____ **16.** We have to bring a lot of equipment to the practice field <u>tomorrow it</u> would be easier to take my car.

  **16.** A) NO CHANGE
       B) tomorrow, it
       C) tomorrow, therefore, it
       D) tomorrow, so it

_____ **17.** Nina's new restaurant buys ingredients from local producers whenever <u>possible, however, some</u> foods just can't be grown outside of a tropical climate.

  **17.** A) NO CHANGE
       B) possible, some
       C) possible; however, some
       D) possible, nevertheless some

_____ **18.** <u>Tensions in Europe were rising on the eve of World War I, no one</u> could have predicted that the sovereignty dispute between Austria and Serbia would lead to a conflict that would embroil the whole continent.

  **18.** A) NO CHANGE
       B) Although tensions in Europe were rising on the eve of World War I, no one
       C) Tensions in Europe had risen on the eve of World War I, no one
       D) Tensions in Europe had risen on the eve of World War I, however no one

_____ **19.** Because Warren loved to swim, he decided to take his vacation in the <u>Caribbean, the water is</u> much clearer and warmer than those near his home in Virginia.

  **19.** A) NO CHANGE
       B) Caribbean, where the water is
       C) Caribbean the water there can be
       D) Caribbean, its waters are

_____ **20.** Terry Gross has been a staple for National Public Radio for over forty <u>years, her</u> show "Fresh Air" continues to be one of the network's most popular programs.

  **20.** A) NO CHANGE
       B) years, and her
       C) years, it is her
       D) years her

**CONTINUE** →

# Writing: Commas 1

_____ **21.** As the lead scientist on the university's new nanobot research <u>team, Dr. Neilson</u> found she spent more time managing the other researchers than doing experiments herself.

**21.** A) NO CHANGE
B) team Dr. Neilson,
C) team, Dr. Neilson,
D) team; Dr. Neilson

_____ **22.** King Leopold II of <u>Belgium, founded a brutally exploitative</u> "Free State" in the Congo by convincing other Europeans that he was engaged in humanitarian work.

**22.** A) NO CHANGE
B) Belgium founded, a brutally exploitative
C) Belgium founded a brutally exploitative
D) Belgium, founded a brutally exploitative,

_____ **23.** John Carpenter's gruesome horror <u>movie *The Thing* made in 1982,</u> is often considered the apex of achievement in practical special effects.

**23.** A) NO CHANGE
B) movie *The Thing* made in 1982
C) movie, *The Thing* made in 1982
D) movie *The Thing*, made in 1982,

_____ **24.** Anybody who knew Stella could tell <u>you that she loved,</u> her dog, her music, and her beat-up pickup truck.

**24.** A) NO CHANGE
B) you that, she loved
C) you, that she loved,
D) you that she loved

_____ **25.** The ascension of Maria Theresa to the throne of <u>Austria, led directly to the War of Austrian Succession,</u> which lasted almost eight years and embroiled most of Europe's great powers.

**25.** A) NO CHANGE
B) Austria led directly to the War of Austrian Succession,
C) Austria led directly, to the War of Austrian Succession
D) Austria, led directly to the War of Austrian Succession

CONTINUE

Name: _____  Date: _____

# Writing: Commas 2

_____ **26.** Andy always preferred to go to the <u>beach, on the north side</u> of the harbor because it was usually less crowded.

**26.** A) NO CHANGE
  B) beach on the north side,
  C) beach, on the north side,
  D) beach on the north side

_____ **27.** Capable of reaching speeds over two hundred miles per <u>hour, the peregrine falcon is the fastest animal on Earth,</u> an honor many mistakenly bestow on the cheetah.

**27.** A) NO CHANGE
  B) hour the peregrine falcon is the fastest animal on Earth,
  C) hour the peregrine falcon is the fastest animal on Earth
  D) hour, the peregrine falcon, is the fastest animal on Earth

_____ **28.** Many of my friends believe that the old mental <u>hospital an abandoned building, across the street, from our school</u> is haunted.

**28.** A) NO CHANGE
  B) hospital, an abandoned building across the street from our school,
  C) hospital, an abandoned building across the street, from our school
  D) hospital an abandoned building, across the street, from our school,

_____ **29.** Melissa's grandfather was a renowned crime-scene <u>photographer, in Chicago, and,</u> she has decorated her apartment with dozens of his most interesting works.

**29.** A) NO CHANGE
  B) photographer, in Chicago and
  C) photographer in Chicago, and
  D) photographer in, Chicago and

_____ **30.** Before he created <u>Mario possibly the most famous video game character of all time,</u> Shigeru Miyamoto was employed by Nintendo to create artwork that would adorn arcade machines.

**30.** A) NO CHANGE
  B) Mario, possibly the most famous video game character of all time,
  C) Mario, possibly, the most famous video game character of all time
  D) Mario, possibly the most famous video game character, of all time

**CONTINUE**

**Name:** _____  **Date:** _____

# Math: Function Notation

**Questions 31 to 36 refer to the following function:**

| Let $h(x) = x^2 + 3x$ |
| --- |

_____ **31.** $h(2) = ?$

    A)    5
    B)    7
    C)    10
    D)    12

_____ **32.** $h(3) = ?$

    A)    6
    B)    9
    C)    12
    D)    18

_____ **33.** $h(-2) = ?$

    A)    $-10$
    B)    $-2$
    C)    $-1$
    D)    10

_____ **34.** $h(7) = ?$

    A)    28
    B)    49
    C)    52
    D)    70

_____ **35.** $h(0) = ?$

    A)    $-3$
    B)    0
    C)    3
    D)    9

_____ **36.** If $h(k) = 0$, which of the following could be the value of $k$?

    A)    $-3$
    B)    $-1$
    C)    3
    D)    9

**Questions 37 to 40 refer to the following function:**

| Let $f(x) = (x - 3)^2$ <br> Let $g(x) = 2x - 1$ |
| --- |

_____ **37.** $f(5) = ?$

    A)    2
    B)    4
    C)    8
    D)    16

_____ **38.** $f(12) = ?$

    A)    9
    B)    18
    C)    27
    D)    81

_____ **39.** $g(8) = ?$

    A)    15
    B)    17
    C)    19
    D)    23

_____ **40.** If $g(4) = a$, what is $f(a)$ ?

    A)    1
    B)    7
    C)    15
    D)    16

**CONTINUE** ➡

*Course D: Homework 4*          – 169 –          *A-List Education*

# Math: Factoring

_____ 41. The expression $(3x - 2)(5x + 8)$ is equivalent to:

A) $15x^2 - 14x - 16$
B) $15x^2 + 14x - 16$
C) $15x^2 - 14x + 16$
D) $15x^2 - 16$

_____ 42. Which of the following expressions is equivalent to $10x^2 + 25x + 15$ ?

A) $(x + 10)(x + 15)$
B) $(x - 1)(10x + 15)$
C) $(x + 1)(10x + 15)$
D) $(x - 1)(15x - 10)$

_____ 43. Which of the following expressions is equivalent to: $16x^2 + 8x + 1 = 0$ ?

A) $(4x + 1)^2$
B) $(4x + 1)(4x - 1)$
C) $(4x - 1)^2$
D) $(1 - 4x)^2$

_____ 44. Which of the following expressions is a factored form of $6xy^5 + 3x^5y$ ?

A) $6x^4y^4$
B) $6xy(y^4 + x^4)$
C) $3xy(2y^4 + x^4)$
D) $3x^4y^4(2y + x)$

_____ 45. Which of the following choices shows all of the positive factors of the number 16?

A) 1, 2, 4, 8, 16
B) 1, 2, 4, 16
C) 1, 2, 4, 12, 32
D) 1, 8, 16, 32

_____ 46. Which of the following expressions is equivalent to $(x + 3)(x^2 + 3x - 5)$ ?

A) $x^3 + 6x^2 + 4x - 15$
B) $x^3 + 3x^2 + 12x - 15$
C) $x^3 + 3x^2 + 9x - 15$
D) $x^3 + 6x^2 + 2x - 15$

_____ 47. Which of the following expressions is equivalent to $6x^2 + 5x - 6$ ?

A) $(3x - 2)(3x + 3)$
B) $(3 - 2x)(2 - 3x)$
C) $(2x - 3)(3x + 2)$
D) $(2x + 3)(3x - 2)$

_____ 48. Which of the following expressions is equivalent to $x^2 - 25$ ?

A) $(x + 5)(x + 5)$
B) $(x + 5)(x - 5)$
C) $(x + 5)^2$
D) $(x - 5)^2$

_____ 49. The expression given below is equivalent to which of the following expressions $8x^2 - 22x - 21$ ?

A) $(2x + 7)(4x - 3)$
B) $(2x - 7)(4x + 3)$
C) $(7x + 2)(3x - 4)$
D) $(7x - 2)(3x + 4)$

_____ 50. Which of the following choices shows all of the positive factors of the number 18?

A) 1, 3, 4, 6, 9, 18
B) 1, 3, 6, 9, 12
C) 1, 2, 6, 9, 36
D) 1, 2, 3, 6, 9, 18

**STOP**

# Homework 5

## Reading: Double Passage 1

**Passage 1**

Not many Americans today can name one living serious composer (though with a little prodding, they might offer up John Williams, noted creator of the music *Line* accompanying the Star Wars movies and other
5 blockbusters). People still attend concerts and operas, but the make-up of the audience doesn't bode well for the future of the art. The average age of a typical concertgoer has been on the rise for decades, and attempts to supplant this graying demographic with younger folks
10 has had limited success, especially from an artistic perspective. Putting together a family-friendly program by including popular songs, movie music, etc., does nothing to further the art form that the orchestras and concert halls were created to serve.

**Passage 2**
15 The current condition of concert music in the U.S. might be described as anemic, with a number of factors contributing to its decline. Ticket prices can be prohibitively high, especially the young. Fewer people of any age play instruments—musically literate non-
20 professionals have long made up a sizable portion of regular concertgoers. But the music itself has to take some of the blame as well. The at-times excruciatingly difficult music that became fashionable in the mid-20$^{th}$ century delivered a body blow to concert attendance that
25 is still being felt. But there is reason for optimism. We've seen a resurgence of ear-pleasing but still adventurous music from a growing clutch of youngish composers. Whether the younger folks who enthusiastically attend concerts of this music can spread the word
30 to those in their demographic who never step foot in a concert hall has yet to be determined.

**MAIN IDEAS:**

A: _____

B: _____

_____ 1. Passages 1 and 2 both make the point that:

A) classical music does not have a sufficiently large audience among young people.
B) fewer classical music fans today listen to music created by young composers.
C) the artistic quality of classical music concerts had been on the decline for years.
D) classical music concerts designed for younger audiences have been unpopular.

_____ 2. Unlike the author of Passage 1, the author of Passage 2:

A) makes the case that attendance at classical music concerts is likely to increase.
B) criticizes composers from the recent past for writing music that was not adventurous.
C) points out that people today are less musically knowledgeable.
D) addresses causes for a decline in interest in classical music.

CONTINUE

# Reading: Double Passage 2

**Passage 1**

Amid the general concern over climate change, there has been less focus on rainforest deforestation. Deforestation, especially in the Amazon, is of course, a significant driver of global warming: the ldeoss of trees, which consume carbon dioxide, leads to greater amounts of carbon in the air, leading in turn to more heat being trapped in Earth's lower atmosphere.

*Line* 5

However, other serious dangers arise from the indiscriminate slash-and-burn approach that continues to be used in the Amazon by loggers and others. The indigenous people have been treated roughly, at times brutally, as their homelands have been destroyed or made uninhabitable. The number of plant and animal species continues to decline at a rate estimated at 50,000 species annually. Deforestation also typically leads to soil erosion, and once fertile areas turn into wasteland.

10

15

**Passage 2**

A number of steps have been taken to curb the serious environmental dangers associated with defor-estation. One of the most common-sense approaches involves a stricter monitoring of forest loss. Arial photographs can be studied by individuals who do not possess advanced training. Satellite images of so-called hot spots, areas most susceptible to rapid loss, can be analyzed. These methods can be used to track regrowth as well as forest loss.

20

25

Another important advance is the development of new farming methods that minimize the amount of deforested land needed by small local farmers by showing them how to increase crop yield. A particularly inventive method for accomplishing this is the creation of food forests that replicate natural forests. These agroforestal systems have proved successful at reducing dependence on fossil fuels and chemicals and improving the quality of the local soil and water. More importantly, this is both a pragmatic and an ethical way to keep in mind the rights of the people who have lived in the forest all their lives.

30

35

**MAIN IDEAS:**

A: _____

B: _____

3.  Both passages mention the people who have always lived in the rainforest, but only Passage 2:

A) involves them in ways to remedy the problem of deforestation.
B) explains how they have helped formulate ways to alleviate the problem of deforestation.
C) states that they have been treated brutally at times in the past.
D) acknowledges that there has been a lessening of habitat loss due to deforestation in recent years.

4.  It can be inferred from the passage that the author of Passage 2 would most likely:

A) feel that the author of Passage 1 has overstated the threat posed by deforestation.
B) strongly agree with the concerns expressed by the author of Passage 1.
C) argue that the solutions proposed by the author of Passage 1 are impractical.
D) point out that climate change is only one threat posed by deforestation.

CONTINUE

# Writing: Apostrophes 1

_____ **5.** The unfortunate nexus of air <u>current's in the office meant Yvonne's</u> desk was always freezing when the air conditioning was active.

**5.** A) NO CHANGE
B) current's in the office meant Yvonnes
C) currents' in the office meant Yvonnes
D) currents in the office meant Yvonne's

_____ **6.** By design, it's difficult to determine where this <u>sentences' apostrophes</u> should be placed.

**6.** A) NO CHANGE
B) sentence's apostrophes
C) sentences apostrophes'
D) sentence's apostrophe's

_____ **7.** The <u>scientists' noses'</u> all wrinkled in unison when confronted with the ghastly results of their attempt to design a new deodorant.

**7.** A) NO CHANGE
B) scientists nose's
C) scientists' noses
D) scientist's noses

_____ **8.** In the raffle, Taylor won a <u>series of cooking lessons from the restaurant's</u> gregarious head chef.

**8.** A) NO CHANGE
B) series of cooking lessons' from the restaurant's
C) series' of cooking lessons from the restaurants
D) series of cooking lesson's from the restaurants

_____ **9.** The <u>neighborhoods criminal elements</u> don't stand a chance against its newest hero!

**9.** A) NO CHANGE
B) neighborhoods' criminal elements
C) neighborhood's criminal elements
D) neighborhoods criminal elements'

CONTINUE

# Writing: Other Punctuation 1

_____ **10.** My friend Naomi—a pediatric surgeon at the local children's <u>hospital,</u> is one of the hardest-working people I know.

**10.** A) NO CHANGE
B) hospital
C) hospital;
D) hospital—

_____ **11.** Simon Bolivar dreamed of a unified and democratic South <u>America, however,</u> in the years immediately after his death, foreign intervention and political infighting quickly dissolved that dream.

**11.** A) NO CHANGE
B) America however;
C) America; however,
D) America, however—

_____ **12.** Before the invention of printing <u>press, creating</u> a new book involved hundreds of hours of meticulous copying by hand, often done by monks.

**12.** A) NO CHANGE
B) press. Creating
C) press: creating
D) press; creating

_____ **13.** Despite the dramatically increasing cost of rent, having increased by more than fifty percent over the last five <u>years—</u>people continue to move to New York City at record rates.

**13.** A) NO CHANGE
B) years,
C) years;
D) years:

_____ **14.** Building new subway lines can be expensive <u>business, if we want to increase capacity and remain in the black,</u> we should focus on refining the service on our existing infrastructure.

**14.** A) NO CHANGE
B) business; if we want to increase capacity and remain in the black;
C) business; if we want to increase capacity and remain in the black,
D) business if we want to increase capacity and remain in the black,

CONTINUE →

# Math: Graphing Functions

_____ **15.** What is the slope of the line that passes through the points $(1, 2)$ and $(3, 8)$ ?

    A)   $-3$
    B)   $-1/3$
    C)   $1/3$
    D)   $3$

_____ **16.** What is the slope of the line that passes through the points $(-6, 4)$ and $(1, -3)$ ?

    A)   $-7/6$
    B)   $-6/7$
    C)   $-1$
    D)   $1$

_____ **17.** What is the $y$-intercept of the line that passes through the points $(1, -1)$ and $(5, 7)$ ?

    A)   $-3$
    B)   $-2$
    C)   $-1$
    D)   $1$

_____ **18.** What is the $x$-intercept of the line that passes through the points $(1, -1)$ and $(5, 7)$ ?

    A)   $1/2$
    B)   $3/2$
    C)   $5/2$
    D)   $7/2$

_____ **19.** The equation of line $\ell$ is $y = 3x + 7$. If line $k$ is perpendicular to line $\ell$, what is the slope of line $k$?

    A)   $-3$
    B)   $-1/3$
    C)   $1/3$
    D)   $3/7$

_____ **20.** The equation of line $\ell$ is $y = 3x - 1$. If line $m$ is the reflection of line $\ell$ across the $x$-axis, what is the slope of line $m$?

    A)   $-3$
    B)   $-1/3$
    C)   $-1$
    D)   $1/3$

_____ **21.** The equation of line $\ell$ is $y = -2x + 3$. If line $k$ is parallel to line $\ell$ and passes through the point $(3,5)$, what is the $y$-intercept of line $k$?

    A)   $8$
    B)   $9$
    C)   $10$
    D)   $11$

**CONTINUE** ➡

_____ **22.** Which of the following could be the graph of

$$y = -\frac{1}{2}x + 2 ?$$

A)                          B)

C)                          D)

_____ **23.** Which of the following could be the graph of
   $y = 2x - 3$ ?

A)                          B)

C)                          D)

_____ **24.** Let the function $f$ be defined by
   $f(x) = ax^2 + bx + c$ where $a$, $b$, and $c$ are
   constants. If $a < 0$ and $c > 0$, then which of the
   following could be the graph of $f$?

A)                          B)

C)                          D)

**STOP**

Name: _____     Date: _____

# Homework 6

## Writing: Redundancy 1

_____ 1.  Every year, our glee club's annual charity benefit raises money to fund music education in poor countries around the world.

1.  A)  NO CHANGE
    B)  Once a year, our
    C)  Our
    D)  As a yearly charity event, our

_____ 2.  Last year my family took a trip to the Netherlands, and I was amazed by the clean public parks there that were so neat.

2.  A)  NO CHANGE
    B)  parks there in the Netherlands.
    C)  tidily there in the Netherlands.
    D)  parks.

_____ 3.  Owen and Logan are pooling their money to buy an advanced digital camera, so they can film the movie script that Owen wrote.

3.  A)  NO CHANGE
    B)  he wrote.
    C)  Owen wrote for a movie.
    D)  was written by him for them to film.

_____ 4.  Isabel knew that she shouldn't open the strange, rumbling box that was making noise in the corner of her grandparent's attic.

4.  A)  NO CHANGE
    B)  odd, rumbling box that was strange
    C)  strange, rumbling box
    D)  odd and strange box

_____ 5.  Pyramids can be found around the world. They were often built by slaves and usually served as religious buildings across the globe.

5.  A)  NO CHANGE
    B)  buildings globally.
    C)  buildings.
    D)  structures anywhere in the world.

CONTINUE ➡

# Writing: Redundancy 2

_____ 6. Stringed instruments played by hand have existed for thousands of years, but the first instruments with recognizable similarities to modern guitars were created in Spain in the 13th century. <u>They have traits in common with modern guitars.</u>

6. A) NO CHANGE
   B) These Spanish instruments share a number of traits with modern guitars.
   C) Modern guitars have a number of similarities to them.
   D) DELETE the underlined portion.

_____ 7. Because his car broke down, all week my friend has found himself in the <u>unfortunate and luckless position</u> of needing to ask his older brother for a ride to work.

7. A) NO CHANGE
   B) unfortunate position
   C) unlucky position for the whole week
   D) lucklessly unfortunate position

_____ 8. Our local tennis <u>club, which serves the nearby area,</u> is planning a tournament for Labor Day weekend.

8. A) NO CHANGE
   B) club
   C) club of tennis players
   D) club, which plays tennis,

_____ 9. Victoria eased past the old marble statue and <u>carefully avoided touching its marble form with great care</u> to prevent it from collapsing.

9. A) NO CHANGE
   B) with great care avoided touching or contacting it
   C) carefully avoided touching it
   D) using great care avoided any contact so as not to touch the statue

_____ 10. Sierra was very proud of her encyclopedic knowledge of mid-nineties television shows and was <u>happy</u> to demonstrate it at parties.

10. A) NO CHANGE
    B) happy and amicable
    C) happy to show and
    D) DELETE the underlined portion.

CONTINUE

# Writing: Transitions 1

_____ 11. Robert the Bald defeated Prince Ethelrood at the Battle of the Three Rivers. He was, <u>however,</u> able to the prince's throne by right of conquest.

11. A) NO CHANGE
    B) nevertheless,
    C) therefore,
    D) previously,

_____ 12. When it comes to running the restaurant, my boss micromanages us way too much. <u>Nevertheless,</u> he makes us account for where every lemon slice goes, and he refuses to let anyone else fold the napkins.

12. A) NO CHANGE
    B) On the other hand,
    C) For example,
    D) Surprisingly,

_____ 13. The Brontë sisters—Charlotte, Emily, and Anne—may very well make up the most talented family of writers in human history. <u>All three</u> enjoyed success as poets and novelists.

13. A) NO CHANGE
    B) However, all three
    C) All three, in contrast,
    D) Therefore, all three

_____ 14. <u>Because</u> the Berlin Wall was brought down more than 25 years ago, differences between the two halves of the city remain.

14. A) NO CHANGE
    B) Although
    C) Before
    D) If

_____ 15. The research team believes there may be a link between low rainfall and the migration routes of geese. <u>For example,</u> they will tag several specimens to track whether the geese appear in areas that have recently experienced drought.

15. A) NO CHANGE
    B) Nevertheless,
    C) Coincidentally,
    D) For this reason,

CONTINUE →

# Writing: Transitions 2

_____ **16.** To celebrate the 4th of July, the city council has planned a giant parade and a million-dollar fireworks spectacle. The whole plan may be in jeopardy, <u>additionally,</u> if this torrential rain refuses to stop.

**16.** A) NO CHANGE
   B) therefore,
   C) for instance,
   D) however,

_____ **17.** Because there is disagreement about what level of soccer counts as "professional", it is difficult to determine the leading scorer of all time. <u>Conversely,</u> some sources name Pelé as having the most goals while others believe it to be Josef Bican.

**17.** A) NO CHANGE
   B) On the other hand,
   C) Consequently,
   D) At that time,

_____ **18.** *Turritopsis dohrnii* is a species of jellyfish that is able to revert from its adult state back to an immature polyp at any time. <u>In light of this ability,</u> the species is called the "immortal jellyfish."

**18.** A) NO CHANGE
   B) Despite this talent,
   C) That is because
   D) Surprisingly, this means

_____ **19.** Theories about the true authorship of Shakespeare's plays are plentiful. In the academic community, <u>therefore,</u> proposed alternative authors are rarely taken seriously, as there is no concrete evidence to suggest any of them wrote the plays.

**19.** A) NO CHANGE
   B) as one example,
   C) similarly,
   D) however,

_____ **20.** At the annual harvest festival, the villagers would bring all their crops to the square to be judged, <u>while</u> those chosen as the finest would be brought to the temple at the top of the mountain.

**20.** A) NO CHANGE
   B) although
   C) during which
   D) after which

CONTINUE

# Math: Technique Review

**DIRECTIONS: You must use an SAT math technique** on each of the following questions. You must indicate which technique you used—either **Plug In** or **Backsolve**—and show your work.

_____ 21. Alvin, Barney, and Cedric made a total of 18 sandwiches to bring to a picnic. Alvin made 2 more sandwiches than Barney made, and Cedric made 3 times as many as Alvin. How many sandwiches did Barney make?

- A) 2
- B) 4
- C) 6
- D) 10

_____ 22. Technique used:

- A) Plug In
- B) Backsolve

_____ 23. If Arthur was $y$ years old exactly 3 years ago, how old will he be in exactly $x$ years?

- A) $x + y$
- B) $x + y - 3$
- C) $x - y - 3$
- D) $x + y + 3$

_____ 24. Technique used:

- A) Plug In
- B) Backsolve

_____ 25. The high road to Scotland is 180 miles longer than the low road. When Jocelyn goes to Scotland by the high road and returns along the low road, the round trip is 1,060 miles. How many miles is the high road?

- A) 350
- B) 440
- C) 530
- D) 620

_____ 26. Technique used:

- A) Plug In
- B) Backsolve

_____ 27. If $a$, $b$, and $c$ are consecutive even integers such that $a < b < c$, which of the following is equal to $a^2 + b^2 + c^2$?

- A) $3b^2 + 2$
- B) $3b^2 + 6$
- C) $3b^2 + 8$
- D) $3b^2 + 6b + 5$

_____ 28. Technique used:

- A) Plug In
- B) Backsolve

_____ 29. It takes Donna 4 minutes to grade an essay, and it takes Clay 6 minutes to grade an essay. If they both start working at the same time, how many minutes will it take them to grade 20 total essays?

- A) 40
- B) 48
- C) 72
- D) 100

_____ 30. Technique used:

- A) Plug In
- B) Backsolve

CONTINUE ➡

# Math: Probability

_____ **31.** A certain jar contains 100 total coins. If 40 of the coins are pennies, what is the probability that a coin chosen at random is a penny?

    A) 1/100
    B) 1/40
    C) 1/25
    D) 2/5

_____ **32.** Gregor has some kittens, 8 of which are grey. If he picks one of his kittens at random, the probability that he chose a grey kitten is 2/3. How many total kittens does Gregor have?

    A) 4
    B) 6
    C) 12
    D) 16

_____ **33.** There are 24 cars in a parking lot. If a car is selected at random, the probability that it is blue is 5/8. How many cars in the parking lot are <u>not</u> blue?

    A) 3
    B) 9
    C) 12
    D) 15

_____ **34.** A store sells shirts in three sizes: Small, Medium, and Large. The store has 11 Small shirts and 7 Medium shirts. If the probability of randomly choosing a Large shirt is 1/3, how many total shirts does the store have?

    A) 6
    B) 9
    C) 18
    D) 27

$$\{ 1, 3, 5, 6, 7, 8, 10, 11, 15, 16 \}$$

_____ **35.** If $k$ is a number chosen at random from the set above, what is the probability that $k$ is divisible by 5?

    A) 1/5
    B) 2/5
    C) 3/9
    D) 3/10

**STOP**

Made in the USA
Middletown, DE
20 October 2023

41161171R00104